Careers in Political Science

Joel Clark

Michigan State University Semester Study Program in Washington, D.C.

PEARSON

Longman

New York Boston San Francisco
London Toronto Sydney Tokyo Singapore Madrid
Mexico City Munich Paris Cape Town Hong Kong Montreal

Careers in Political Science

Copyright ©2004 Pearson Education

Cover Designer/Manager: Wendy Ann Fredericks

Cover Photos: © BananaStock/ BananaStock, Ltd / PictureQuest; © Jason Reed / Getty Images, Inc./ © Dynamic Graphics, Inc.

ISBN: 0321-11337-3

2 3 4 5 6 7 8 9 10-PH –06 05 04

Dedication

To John and Patricia Clark, for always supporting my career decisions, and to Ava Helene, who became my full-time career during the writing of this book.

Preface

Colleges and universities are supposed to help students explore new ideas, develop lifelong learning skills and prepare for productive careers after graduation. Yet, schools can't do everything. Students must also take responsibility for managing their own futures. Unfortunately, this often doesn't happen. Each semester too many students learn the hard way that adequate career preparation can't start after graduation. *Careers in Political Science* is written for those who already declared political science as their major, for those who are considering political science, and for those who advise students about academic majors and careers. Students in related majors including public administration, communications and liberal arts can also benefit from this book.

The purpose of *Careers in Political Science* is to help students explore various careers associated with political science and to develop realistic career strategies while they are in school. Although other resources about political science are available, this book strives to address the common concerns of real students and to humanize a subject that is often presented in a dry manner. Each chapter provides a general overview of a career field commonly associated with political science, and lists various print and electronic resources to help students conduct more in-depth research. More importantly, each chapter dispels many faulty (and often false) beliefs about that career field, and tests students' assumptions about what they want to do and how they can achieve their goals. Finally, while *Careers in Political Science* provides the latest salary and employment trends available, and utilizes the advice of experts in many fields, it doesn't rely solely on these sources. Instead, through numerous career profiles it reveals the experiences and insights of real people who were once where the book's readers are now. The hope is that students will identify with one or more of these people and take to heart their invaluable examples and lessons.

Acknowledgements

The author wishes to thank those who shared their personal examples and insights in the career profiles found throughout this book: Don Beezley, Gerrie Benedi, Linda Blauhut, Ernie Chung, Simonas Girdzijauskas, Lisa Havlovitz, Donald Leonard, Ben Murphy, Susan Oglinsky, Russell Phipps, Maria Pica, Brian Reznick, John Seymour, Ana Tolentino, Edward Villacorta, Nick Warner, Brianna Wilkins, and Lisa Zabawa. A special thanks also goes to those who provided advice in the book on one or more topics, or information or suggestions during the project's research phase: Nona Anderson, Dave Bauer, Larry Berman, Marty Carcieri, Diane Hensel, Madina Ishmukhamedova, Melody Johnson, LuAnn Miller, Vicki Robinson, Steve Selby, Dale Slaght, Sonja Taylor, and Pat Lewis. Finally, the author thanks Eric Stano and Kristi Olson at Longman, and the anonymous reviewers who read earlier drafts of the manuscript:
Barron Boyd, Le Moyne College
John Walton Cotman, Howard University
Ellen Grigsby, University of New Mexico
Kim Q. Hill, Texas A&M University
Robin Kolodny, Temple University
Brett S. Sharp, University of Central Oklahoma
E. Ike Udogu, Francis Marion University
Their input improved the final draft in numerous ways. Of course, any remaining omissions or other weaknesses are the sole responsibility of the author.

About the Author

Joel Clark earned his Ph.D. in political science from the University of California, Santa Barbara. He is Washington Director of Michigan State University's Semester Study Program in Washington, D.C, and author of *Intern to Success* (2002). In addition to writing on careers and internships, Professor Clark's research interests include American political reform and state activities in international affairs.

Table of Contents

1. Introduction

Undergraduate political science programs—or their equivalent, including government, politics, and public affairs—usually rank among the top academic majors at most schools in terms of students enrolled and degrees awarded. This is not surprising since political science explores topics that affect people directly. Politics matters, and like it or not government continues to play an important role in everyone's lives, both in the United States and abroad.

Most students first choose political science because of their general interest in domestic or international politics, law or current affairs, not because of their detailed understanding of the career options available to them. A common refrain that political science majors often hear is: "Political science is interesting, but what can you do with it?" The answer should be: "A lot!" *Careers in Political Science* can help students answer this question with confidence.

Graduates with political science degrees have traditionally enjoyed solid career options in various fields including government, nonprofit management, interest advocacy, international affairs, campaigns, elections, law, and teaching. But your career options don't have to fit neatly into these categories. A cursory survey of alumni from political science programs shows that political science graduates are found in every career field imaginable, including banking, television production, counseling, and information technology.[i] While some individuals holding these positions completed graduate studies or further training, this list should begin to dispel the myth that holding a political science degree limits a person's career options.

---

[i] A review of several political science department websites shows that graduates with political science degrees work in almost every conceivable career. Actual positions held by political science graduates include: Program Planning Analyst with EPA; Director of Safe Communities with the State of Maryland; Executive Vice President with Gettysburg Health Care Corp.; Contractor with MCI Communications; Public Relations Coordinator with Visa International; Account Manager with Armstrong World Industries; Language Instructor at the Japanese Embassy; Program Manager with The NEED Project; Policy Director with the National Immigration Forum; Lobbyist with the National Right to Work Group; Community Development Director with the National Coalition for Advanced Manufacturing; Interactive Media Developer with AOL Times Warner; and Logistics Officer with the CIA.

Another way to consider the issue of career paths for political science majors is to recognize some of the more famous people who hold political science degrees. These include social activist Gloria Steinem, broadcast journalist Jane Pauley, CEO of America Online, Steve Case, actors Alec and William Baldwin, and politician and talk show host Jerry Springer. The many political science majors who have built successful careers in politics or public affairs include Representatives Geraldine Ferraro and Barbara Jordan, Health and Human Services Secretary Margaret Heckler, Chief Justice Earl Warren, Secretary of State Madeleine Albright, and Presidents Woodrow Wilson, John Kennedy and Lyndon Johnson.[1]

How This Book Can Help You
While political science graduates are found in all job sectors, the careers identified in this book are closely related to the topics and skills that are likely covered in your political science major. *Careers in Political Science* is written for those who already declared political science as their major, for those who are considering political science, and for those who advise students about academic majors and careers. Each chapter contains specific job descriptions, employment statistics and real-person profiles. Additional print and web resources are listed at the end of each chapter to help you do more research in those areas you find most interesting.

Because adequate career preparation is a cumulative process, you shouldn't wait until your senior year to begin thinking seriously about what you are doing in college, and what you will do when you graduate. In today's competitive career environment it's never too early to begin exploring your career options, and making the most of your college years. *Careers in Political Science* will help you get the most out of your political science education, and to eventually make the successful transition toward a rewarding career.

Political Science: A Long and Honorable Academic Tradition
In choosing to study political science you are embarking on a long and honorable academic tradition. Debate and study about politics played an important role in the development of the first human societies. The ancient Greeks, for example, were the first civilization to rank political science among the highest academic disciplines. Aristotle (384BC-322BC) considered political science "the queen of all sciences" because he believed that human knowledge and development were possible only

through the *polis*, or political community. In his *Politics*, Aristotle systematically explored the nature of political societies and speculated on their just and corrupt forms. Because Aristotle's methods of inquiry included systematic observation of actual political phenomena, and not just philosophical ideals, he is widely considered to be the first "political scientist." Aristotle and his students categorized approximately 350 Greek constitutions, and made logical assertions about the best regimes possible given local histories, cultures, economies, and geographical conditions. Political scientists still study the Greeks because they thought deeply about many of the same political issues we grapple with today.

Nicolo Machiavelli (1469-1527) is generally considered the first "modern" political scientist. For many years Machiavelli served as a high level administrator during the Medici family's rule in Venice. Machiavelli's primary concern was not the best state (the Greek's general concern), but the best attainable state given the unstable domestic and international political conditions of his time. Simply put, Machiavelli preferred to focus on the art of the possible. In *The Prince*, he offers the political ruler practical advice on how he can enhance his personal power and interests, and hence the interests of the state.

Subsequent political writers in the seventeenth and eighteenth centuries, including Thomas Hobbes, John Locke and Jean-Jacques Rousseau attempted to develop conceptions of state sovereignty that derived more directly from popular consent. Their writings shaped the political attitudes of English, American and French Revolutionaries. Central figures in America's founding generation, including John Adams, James Madison, Thomas Jefferson and Alexander Hamilton, were well schooled in political history and theory. They succeeded in transforming the theoretical works of past political thinkers into a "new science of politics"[2] that culminated in the ratification of the U.S. Constitution.

Political science became a formal academic discipline in the United States after the Civil War with the creation of graduate programs at various schools including Johns Hopkins University and Columbia College (later Columbia University). In 1903, the American Political Science Association (APSA) was established to promote the interests of those who study political science. The first issue of the *American Political Science Review* was printed in 1906. Woodrow Wilson, who earned a doctorate in Political Science from Johns Hopkins University, became the eighth president of the APSA in 1911, and later served two terms as President of the United States.[3]

Political Science today offers a rich mixture of theoretical and empirical approaches to countless public issues. Some political scientists prefer to utilize the latest social science methods, including modeling and multivariate analysis, while others rely more on traditional philosophical approaches. Basic questions that preoccupy political scientists and their students include: What are the best political arrangements to promote freedom, equality and the consent of the governed? What does it mean to be a "citizen" in a democratic republic? How can societies become or remain democratic in times of rapid demographic and technological change? How do individuals, groups and states behave under various social economic and political conditions? What are the contours of democracy and democratic development in countries around the globe, and among sub-national peoples with different ethnic, religious and socioeconomic histories?

The discipline of political science is built upon a core of basic introductory concepts and methods, and includes an extensive menu of sub-fields that offer something for just about everyone. Many political science programs are organized around the following fields of study:

American Government and Politics
International and Comparative Politics
Normative and Formal Theory
Public Law
Public Policy and Administration

Students generally complete a combination of introductory and advance courses that span several major fields. Once students complete their compulsory courses they usually have the option of concentrating in one or more sub-fields. The following list of organized panel sections from the 2002 meeting of the American Political Science Association [4] describes the range of sub-specialties within political science:
Political Thought and Philosophy: Historical Approaches
Foundations of Political Theory
History of Political Theory
Formal Political Theory
Political Psychology

Political Economy
Politics and History
Political Methodology
Teaching and Learning in Political Science
Undergraduate Education
Comparative Politics
Comparative Politics of Developing Countries
Politics of Communist and Former Communist Countries
Comparative Politics of Advanced Industrial Societies
European Politics and Society
International Political Economy
International Collaboration
International Security
International Security and Arms Control
Foreign Policy
Conflict Processes
Legislative Studies
Presidency Research
Public Administration
Public Policy
Law and Courts
Constitutional Law and Jurisprudence
Federalism and Intergovernmental Relations
State Politics and Policy
Urban Politics
Women and Politics
Race, Ethnicity and Politics
Religion and Politics
Representation and Electoral Systems
Political Organizations and Parties
Elections and Voting Behavior
Public Opinion and Political Participation
Political Communications
Science, Technology and Environmental Politics
Information Technology and Politics
Politics and Literature
New Political Science
Ecological and Transformational Politics
International History and Politics
Comparative Democratization

Human Rights

Your professors in political science will undoubtedly specialize in one or more of these areas. Perhaps you will choose to specialize yourself, and work to advance our understanding of these topics through your research papers, class projects, independent studies, and other forms of faculty and student collaboration.

Career Preparation: Not Just Taking Classes
A major purpose of this book is to help you make the most of your political science education. In today's competitive job markets it's not enough to study hard and graduate with a strong grade point average (GPA). To succeed you must also develop a learning and career strategy that reflects your values and interests. While the transition from college to career has never been a "one size fits all" process, today the emphasis is even more on your individual skills and experiences, and less on the common benefits of one particular major over another. A well-prepared college graduate possesses solid classroom skills (e.g., reading, writing, analytical reasoning), some specialized skills learned through electives or a minor (e.g., foreign language, computer software proficiency, or advanced research skills), and workplace skills attained through part-time work, internships and extracurricular activities (e.g., customer service and the ability to handle several projects simultaneously). As Dave Bauer, Manager of Technical Resources for IBM Global Services puts it: "As a job applicant you have to have something the employer is interested in. What the employer is interested in is a hard skill."[5]

This is not to say that your choice of major is totally irrelevant. It obviously isn't. Students do better in majors that interest them. And whether you like it or not, your GPA is one measure of educational success, and a major determinant for whether you will later qualify for scholarships or other merit-based awards, or gain admission to graduate or law school. Many students drop out of other majors because they are not interested in those subjects, and consequently struggle in their classes. They switch to political science because they are drawn to the subjects taught in political science classes, and want to learn more about those topics. It is important to choose a major that particularly interests you, not one that others think is best for you, or one you think will land you the most prestigious job after graduation.

Generally, the best path to academic success is to remain intellectually challenged and personally engaged in your studies. The best path to a rewarding career is to supplement your classroom learning with additional skill development and real work experiences. The following chapters will identify the keys to intellectual growth and career development in various career sectors associated with political science. Before we examine those sectors, it will be useful to first think carefully about who you are as a person, and what interests you.

---

[1] Examples found at <www.regisnet.regiscollege.edu/polisci/careers.html>.

[2] For the classic statement of this "new science," as applied to the U.S. Constitution, see Alexander Hamilton, James Madison, and John Jay, *The Federalist* (1788).

[3] For a thoughtful and sometimes critical history of the development of political science as a formal discipline, see David M. Ricci, *The Tragedy of Political Science*. New Haven: Yale University Press (1984).

[4] <www.apsanet.org/mtgs/divisions/index.cfm>.

[5] Interview with the author.

2. Self-Assessment: A Useful First Step

What interests you? History, languages, law, media, travel?
What kind of person are you? An independent thinker, or someone who tends to follow the crowd? An introvert? An extrovert?
How do you work best? In teams, or alone? Under strict deadlines, or at your own pace?
What do you value most in life? Stability? Helping others? Making money? Being creative?

These are some typical questions that career guidance professionals will ask you when you seek their advice about possible careers. It's never too early to begin exploring these and related questions about yourself. Even though graduation from college may seem light years away, it isn't. Your college years will pass by quickly. You can bet on it. Simply put, you must know yourself to know what you want, and you must know what you want before you can work toward your goals. A thorough self-assessment can help you identify your personal traits and unique interests. To be useful, your personal evaluation requires an honest examination of your values, interests and existing developed and undeveloped skills.

At this point you might be thinking: "All this sounds great. But I have <u>no</u> idea what I want to do with the rest of my life." Guess what? That's okay, at least for now. This book assumes that most students don't have a clear idea about what they want to do, and many may not know even at graduation. Each year thousands of students graduate from college without a plan for the rest of their lives (be warned, this fact might disturb your friends and family members!), and many will make several career changes before they settle on a sustained career path. Most of us have tried out new jobs, reassessed our career assumptions, or had to react to changing work environments. The best strategy at this point is to be as proactive in your career development as you can. Even if you don't know what you want to do after graduation there are still things you can do now to prepare for future career success.

Initial Advice For Students With Clear Educational and Career Goals
Some students already have strong ideas about their chosen career. Their main choices involve what classes to take, how to strengthen their undeveloped skills, and how to gain valuable work experiences. Typical advice for these students will include participating in departmental and

campus activities, exploring internships and study-abroad opportunities, and working closely with their campus career center to develop job-seeking skills. If you have clear career goals this book can help you be more strategic in making your educational and career choices.

Ironically, it's often those students who believe they know exactly what they want who need further career guidance the most. Students with firm goals are more apt to close themselves off to other opportunities. While it's good to have a clear direction, it also pays to remain open to options you haven't considered, and to continue to test your assumptions in classes, internships, and other activities. Among the many successful people profiled in this book, several found out the hard way that their first-choice career wasn't as glamorous or rewarding as they initially thought, while others stumbled onto opportunities they hadn't considered at first. Think about what these people have to say, and consider how their experiences might apply to your educational and career development. As you pursue your degree, try to remain open to new possibilities and ways of thinking. You have nothing to lose, and possibly a lot to gain. If your current career plans are right for you, they will hold up over the long run.

Initial Advice For Students Who Don't Have Clear Educational or Career Goals
If you are not sure about what you want to do, don't stress over it. Many people who now enjoy great careers didn't start out with a clear plan on how to get there. Listen carefully to successful people as they discuss their educational and career paths. They typically started out pursuing one thing and along the way shifted their plans in response to chance opportunities or other circumstances (both fortunate and unfortunate). The key is to stay focused on developing the skills and knowledge that are useful for various careers.

Of course, there is a difference between being open and flexible, and being totally aimless. Students who can't decide on an academic major, or who frequently jump from one major to another often take longer to complete their degrees. And those who can't decide at all are "at risk" for dropping out of school completely. Most of us can remember how it felt to sit in long (and sometimes boring) classes and think: "What am I doing here? How will I apply this information later in life?" Despite these doubts you should resist the temptation to drop out of school. As you take more classes in political science, interesting ideas and possibilities are bound to emerge.

For a few individuals there may be times when delaying college is appropriate. But for those who have the aptitude, it always pays to finish the degree. According to a study by the American Council on Higher Education, 77 percent of adults surveyed believe that a college education today is more important than it was ten years ago.[1] In addition, evidence suggests that a college education can help insulate you from periodic slumps in the economy. The Employment Policy Foundation, for example, reported that while 1.9 million Americans without a college degree recently lost their jobs, 1.2 million people with college or vocational degrees were actually hired during the same period.[2] If you prefer to focus on the economic bottom line, consider this: The U.S. Census Bureau reports that the average annual salary of workers who hold high school diplomas is $26,000, compared to $40,000 for those with a bachelor's degree, and $50,000 for those who hold a master's degree.[3] These are strong economic incentives to stick it out and complete your degree.

The career fields described in this book vary widely in terms of their workplace environments, their predominant tasks and projects, and the skills and experiences they require of new applicants. Campaign managers, for example, tend to be self-starters who work in an unstructured environment. Government employees, on the other hand, often have predictable schedules and well-defined tasks. Program managers in nonprofit organizations work in a variety of office cultures with varying expectations. Your choice of a career field should be informed by careful consideration of who you are, what you value, and how you work best.

The following exercises can help you begin the necessary process of self-examination. For further help, consult the websites and print resources listed at the end of this chapter. Also, make an appointment today to visit your school's career center; you will be glad you did.

Exploring Your Personal Traits

Your personal traits[4] help determine who you are. To help you identify your prominent personal traits, write down ten words from Exhibit 1 that best describe you.[5] At this point don't worry about whether these traits are positive or negative, and don't rank them in importance. What do your chosen terms say about you? Do you discern any patterns that might be relevant for your career choices? How consistent are your selections? Presumably, people with very strong or well-developed personality traits may find that their choices reinforce each other. For example, if you chose *adventurous* and *determined* you might also have selected *industrious, open-minded* and *resourceful*. Someone with strong but very different traits might choose items like *cautious, conservative, introverted, patient* and *self-disciplined*.

Exhibit 1. Personal Traits

Accurate	Dominant	Innovative	Poised	Silly
Active	Eager	Intellectual	Polite	Sincere
Adaptable	Easygoing	Intelligent	Practical	Sociable
Adventurous	Efficient	Introverted	Precise	Spiritual
Aggressive	Emotional	Intuitive	Principled	Spontaneous
Ambitious	Empathetic	Inventive	Private	Strong
Analytical	Energetic	Jovial	Productive	Strong-minded
Artistic	Excitable	Just	Progressive	Structured
Boisterous	Expressive	Kind	Quick	Subjective
Bold	Extroverted	Laid-back	Quiet	Tactful
Boring	Fair	Liberal	Quirky	Tentative
Brave	Farsighted	Likable	Rational	Thorough
Calm	Feeling	Logical	Realistic	Thoughtful
Capable	Firm	Loyal	Receptive	Tolerant
Caring	Flexible	Mature	Reflective	Trusting
Cautious	Formal	Methodical	Relaxed	Trustworthy
Cheerful	Friendly	Meticulous	Reliable	Truthful
Clean	Fun	Mistrustful	Reserved	Understanding
Competent	Future-oriented	Modest	Resourceful	Unexcitable
Confident	Generous	Motivated	Responsible	Uninhibited
Conscientious	Gentle	Objective	Responsive	Unmotivated
Conservative	Genuine	Observant	Reverent	Vain
Considerate	Good-natured	Open-minded	Sedentary	Verbal
Cool	Gregarious	Opportunistic	Self-confident	Versatile
Cooperative	Helpful	Optimistic	Self-controlled	Whimsical
Courageous	Honest	Organized	Self-critical	Wholesome
Critical	Humorous	Original	Self-disciplined	Wise
Curious	Idealistic	Patient	Self-reliant	
Daring	Imaginative	Peaceable	Sensible	
Decisive	Impersonal	Perceptive	Sensitive	
Deliberate	Independent	Persistent	Serious	
Detail-oriented	Individualistic	Personable		
Determined	Industrious	Persuasive		
Discreet	Informal	Pleasant		

If your choices don't seem consistent or self-reinforcing, don't worry. It may be that your personality traits are less established, or that you haven't had the right types of experiences to bring them out.

Your Personal Values

Your personal values help define what you value most in life, and what activities you find more rewarding and worthwhile than others. Generally the more your activities reinforce your personal values, the more you will feel satisfied with your work obligations and in control of your life. Review the list of personal values in Exhibit 2.[6] Rank each item in terms of importance using the following scale: 1 = very important, 2 = somewhat important, 3 = not important.

Exhibit 2. Personal Values

Good health	Community	Leadership
Close friendships	Leisure time	Physical appearance
Fulfilling career	Stable life	Physical activities
Stable marriage	Religious values	Exciting life
Financial comfort	Social change	Politics
Independence	Recognition	Strong moral values
Creativity	Helping others	Teaching
Religion	Choice of residence	Writing to influence
Having children	Time to myself	Being famous
Lifestyle freedom	Cultural activities	Making money
Home ownership	Challenging life	
Loving relationship	Frequent change	

What do those items you rank "most important" suggest about your possible choice of career? What do those you rank as least important say about you, and the goals you may choose to pursue? As you read this book, try to match your predominant values to the positive and negative values associated with different career fields. For example, teaching is generally not associated with *making a lot of money* (although teachers' salaries are getting better), but teaching is associated with other work values such as *leadership opportunities* and *helping others*.

Now group your "most important" values into those that are attainable in the near future, and those that will have to come later. *Making a lot of money*, or *being famous*, for example, may have to wait until you finish school and gain more work experience, while *helping others* or *community involvement* are surely more attainable in the short run. Also identify those values you have already fulfilled, and begin to consider how you might work towards the others.

Exploring Your Work Values
Your work values stem from a unique mixture of interests, motivations, and preferred activities. The following vocational themes are adapted from the theories of John Holland.[7] Rank these themes in terms of which are most appealing to you, less appealing, and least appealing. As you learn new information about the career options presented in this book, refer back to these themes to explore possible matches with your predominant work values.

Realistic—Expresses interests and solves problems by *Doing*.
Enjoys working with machines, tools, objects and animals. Is practical, reserved and physical. Likes to work outdoors on concrete problems and see tangible results.

Investigative—Expresses interests and solves problems by *Thinking*.
Enjoys researching, exploring ideas, and collecting data. Is inquiring and analytical. Is methodological, original and logical.

Artistic—Expresses interests and solves problems by *Creating*.
Enjoys being original and independent. Is introspective, self-expressive, innovative, and unstructured.

Social—Expresses interests and solves problems by *Helping*.
Enjoys working with people to inform, train, enlighten, or cure. Is perceptive, responsible, emphatic, patient and responsible.

Enterprising—Expresses interests and solves problems by *Persuading*.
Enjoys using the mind, words, and feelings to deal with and motivate people. Likes to persuade, manage, and sell things or promote ideas. Isn't afraid to take personal or financial risks.

Conventional—Expresses interests and solves problems by *Organizing*.
Enjoys activities that permit organization of information in a clear, orderly manner. Is detail-oriented, responsible, and conforming. Prefers structured settings.

Issues Versus Skills

As you think further about the types of careers that are most compatible with your personal values, consider the possible differences between your interests in issues versus your interest in using certain skills. Some people are driven more by the issues they care about. Your interest in issues might include things like economic development, environmental policy or human rights. If so, you might consider a career in an international nonprofit organization that promotes human rights, or in an "environmentally friendly" corporation.

Other people are more motivated by using the skills they have developed. Your interest in certain skills, for example, might include persuasive writing or language translation. If so, you might consider working for a policy think tank, or for a government agency that is involved in international affairs. Some skills, such as those involving communications (e.g., grant writing, speech writing, public relations), computer proficiency (e.g., web design, database management), or fundraising are valued in a variety of public or private sector career fields. For many people, the particular "mission" of their organization is less important than the opportunity to do the things they like to do.

At this point in your education it pays to develop your skills and interests simultaneously. As Pat Lewis, Nonprofit Management Professional at George Mason University, explains:

> Your work in any organization must be motivated by its mission, narrowly or broadly defined. For example, 'making the world a better place,' or 'finding housing for senior citizens.' At the same time, you can apply your interests and skills to a variety of areas. If your broad interest is education, you can work for an educational foundation, or a performing arts center. Find a place where you can match your skills to your heart, but don't narrow your heart too much because you never know where learning can take place within an organization.[8]

Now that you have thought more carefully about who you are, what interests you, and what you value, it's time to examine several career fields traditionally associated with the study of political science.

Additional Resources
There are many excellent print and electronic resources available to help you conduct a more thorough self-assessment. Useful books include:

- *What Color is Your Parachute?* Richard Bolles. Ten Speed Press (2003).

- *Cool Careers for Dummies.* Marty Nemko, Paul Edwards and Sarah Edwards. John Wiley & Sons (2001).

- *Discover What You're Best At.* Linda Gale. Fireside (1998).

Useful web resources include:

- General and specific guidance for identifying your skills and interests, by Janis Whisman, 1996. Found at <www.regis.edu/spsmnm/jobbook.htm >.

- Career One Stop is a publicly funded resource for job seekers and employers that includes information on job sectors, salaries and career trends. Found at <www.careeronestop.org>.

- The Bureau of Labor Statistics website, which includes updated salary information and job descriptions for many career sectors, is found at <www.bls.gov>.

---

[1] Study entitled: "Attitudes Toward Public Higher Education," reported in the *Chronicle of Higher Education*, 2-6-2000.

[2] Period examined, September 2000 and October 2001. As reported in Daniel Eisenberg, "The Coming Job Boom," *Time*, 5-6-02.

[3] As reported in "The Job Market for the Class of 2000," *Job Choices Diversity Edition, 2002*. National Association of Colleges and Employers, p. 28.

[4] Some material in these assessments is derived from Joel Clark, *Intern to Success*. Boston: Houghton Mifflin (2002).

[5] The list of personal traits was derived from exercises in Blythe Camenson, *Great Jobs for Liberal Arts Majors,* New York: McGraw-Hill (2002), and Richard Nelson Bolles, *What Color is Your Parachute?* Ten Speed Press (2001).

[6] The list of personal values was adapted from Bernadette M. Black and Fred J. Hecklinger, *Training for Life: A Practical Guide to Career and Life Planning,* 7th ed., (2000), and *Moving On: A Guide for Career Planning and Job Search,* University Career Services, George Mason University (2001).

[7] See the Gary D. Gottledeson and John Holland, *Dictionary of Holland Occupational Codes.* Odessa, Fla: PAR, Inc. (1989). Also adapted from *Moving On.*

[8] Interview with the author.

3. Federal Government

In his January 1961, inaugural speech, President John Kennedy declared: "Ask not what your country can do for you—ask what you can do for your country." With these words President Kennedy inspired a whole generation of young people to public service. That generation is beginning to retire at a time when the need for public-sector workers remains acute. America faces new challenges posed by a war on terrorism and its increasingly complex role in world affairs. In response to these new challenges, President George W. Bush has renewed the call for young people to serve, and evidence suggests that at least in the national security realm people are answering that call. But in the next few years hundreds of thousands of additional workers will be needed across all sectors of the federal government, domestic and international.

The looming shortage of federal employees offers great opportunities for students who are now in school. Your political science courses can help you develop a solid knowledge of the origins and development of government, including the numerous varieties of governmental units as well as the broad reach of government programs. In your classes you will also examine problems involving government operations, political struggles between levels of government, and the basic intricacies of public administration and policymaking.

What do federal government workers do? Simply put, they do everything that private sector workers do, and more. Federal employees hold positions as accountants, administrative assistants, bookkeepers, librarians computer specialists, data analysts, lawyers, project managers, communications specialists, and countless other titles.

A Brief History and Overview of the Federal Workforce
The early 1990s were not the best of times for federal workers. Many politicians ran for election by portraying government employees as entrenched bureaucrats who were more interested in solidifying their positions within the bureaucracy than in solving real problems. While critics raised valid claims about the inefficiency of the government, their perceptions were often distorted and overblown. Most government workers are dedicated and productive professionals. Moreover, despite the rhetoric about government being the problem, the truth is that government programs matter to real people.
This period represents one of several waves of anti-government sentiment in American history. While skepticism of government's power and reach is a healthy part of our political culture, taken too far it distorts our understanding of who government workers are, and what they do. For example, many Americans mistakenly believe that most federal employees work "inside the beltway" in Washington, DC, when in reality the

majority of the federal workforce is located outside Washington in communities across America and abroad.

Another mistaken assumption is that the federal workforce is less efficient than its private-sector counterpart. This comparison is invalid for several reasons. First, government programs provide many essential public goods and services--including veteran's benefits, food safety standards, and national defense--that may not be fully provided in an exclusive for-profit economy. Second, government managers are dependent on varying and uncertain budget support from elected officials, and often lack the authority needed to hire or lay off employees or make other decisive program changes. Third, recent examples of large-scale corporate failures suggest that private or publicly held for-profit organizations can be just as inefficient as government, sometimes more so. Finally, as reformers sought to slash government programs in the 1990s, a public backlash ensued where beneficiaries of the programs protested the cuts. National crises including Hurricane Andrew in Florida, or the more recent war on terrorism, reaffirm the central role that government plays in our lives. It turns out that government matters after all.

Whether or not the federal workforce can continue to meet these new challenges remains to be seen. The federal sector is now experiencing a severe recruiting and retention crisis that promises to get worse before it gets better. More than half of the current 1.8 million-member civilian workforce will be eligible to retire by 2004.[1] As Daniel Eisenberg puts it, "[f]rom the Food and Drug Administration (FDA) and Park Service, to the Commerce, Energy and State Departments, agencies are bracing for a brain drain, especially at the management level."[2] Federal agencies are now scrambling to devise innovative ways to attract and keep good employees by developing new internship and training programs, simplifying hiring procedures, and adding benefits including flextime options and educational tuition assistance. While more must be done to make federal careers a desirable option for young people, improvements in hiring and retention will undoubtedly continue.

Because federal departments and agencies perform an enormous variety of tasks, it's impossible to describe in a few lines the myriad opportunities open to political science graduates. The resource list at the end of this chapter includes website information for many departments and agencies so that you can research their various missions, projects and job titles. A special list of websites also points to internships and other student work opportunities. To begin exploring whether federal employment may be right for you, it will be useful to first consider how the federal government hires and promotes most of its employees.

The Civil Service System

Most federal workers are employed through the Civil Service system, which maintains standardized hiring, salary and promotion procedures for most federal departments and agencies. Traditionally, the application process for Civil Service positions was cumbersome and lengthy. The Office of Personnel Management (OPM), the main federal personnel agency, is devising ways to simplify the application process to make federal careers more attractive to qualified applicants.

Salary levels for the Civil Service are determined through the General Schedule (GS) system. Actual salaries depend on a person's job type, with clerical jobs paying less and professional jobs requiring expertise paying more. The following chart illustrates the range of salary steps within each GS pay grade, as of January 1, 2002. Many entry-level federal jobs open to political science graduates will start in the GS 6 through 9 range, although some new full-time hires may start lower or higher.

2002 General Schedule Pay Rates
Annual Rates by Grade and Step

GS	1	2	3	4	5	6	7	8	9	10
1	14757	15249	15740	16228	16720	17009	17492	17981	18001	18456
2	16592	16985	17535	18001	18201	18736	19271	19806	20341	20876
3	18103	18706	19309	19912	20515	21118	21721	22324	22927	23530
4	20322	20999	21676	22353	23030	23707	24384	25061	25738	26415
5	22737	23495	24253	25011	25769	26527	27285	28043	28801	29559
6	25344	26189	27034	27879	28724	29569	30414	31259	32104	32949
7	28164	29103	30042	30981	31920	32859	33798	34737	35676	36615
8	31191	32231	33271	34311	35351	36391	37431	38471	39511	40551
9	34451	35599	36747	37895	39043	40191	41339	42487	43635	44783
10	37939	39204	40469	41734	42999	44264	45529	46794	48059	49324
11	41684	43073	44462	45851	47240	48629	50018	51407	52796	54185
12	49959	51624	53289	54954	56619	58284	59949	61614	63279	64944
13	59409	61389	63369	65349	67329	69309	71289	73269	75249	77229
14	70205	72545	74885	77225	79565	81905	84245	86585	88925	91265
15	82580	85333	88086	90839	93592	96345	99098	101851	104604	107357

Source: GovExec.com

The USAJobs website is OPM's main resource for those seeking a job in the federal government. Located at <www.usajobs.opm.gov>, it includes automated job listings for all departments, agencies, and offices throughout the U.S. and abroad, employment fact sheets, job applications and related forms, and an online resume development program.

Alternative Federal Hiring Programs
In addition to regular Civil Service employment, many federal agencies sponsor separate employment categories to accommodate part-time or limited-duration workers, or to provide training or other opportunities for college students. Increasingly, the federal government is finding innovative ways to attract college students and expose them to federal job opportunities. Student employment programs that already exist include:

Federal Career Intern Program This program is designed to attract exceptional college students and recent graduates into various federal agencies. Generally, interns are hired at the GS levels of 5 through 9, depending on the agency and the applicant's qualifications, and are usually appointed for two years.

Student Temporary Education Program (STEP) The STEP program provides temporary employment opportunities for registered college students. Employment doesn't necessarily have to be related to a student's academic program.
Summer Employment Program Open to students and non-students, this program is designed for those who can only work during the summer months. It provides a wide variety of training and work opportunities.

Volunteer Programs Many unpaid work opportunities are available to students and non-students. If you can manage to temporarily work for free, these programs provide good opportunities to "try out" various occupations and agencies and gain valuable work experience.

For more details on these federal student programs, go to <www.usajobs.opm.gov>.

Presidential Management Intern Program (PMI) Administered by the U.S. Office for Personnel Management, the PMI places students with graduate degrees into various management positions in federal departments and agencies. Many alumni of PMI now hold high-ranking positions in the federal government. For further information, go to <www.pmi.opm.gov>.

AmeriCorps AmeriCorps employs more than 50,000 citizens each year in a variety of national service programs involving education, public safety, health, and the environment. To qualify, applicants must be U.S. citizens, nationals, or lawful permanent residents aged 17 or older. Full-time participants serve from 10-12 months and receive an education award of $4,725 to pay for college, graduate school, or to pay back student loans. The program also provides health insurance, training, and student loan deferments. For more information, go to <www.americorps.org>.

Career Profile: Lisa Zabawa

Lisa Zabawa worked as a paid intern in the Washington office of the U.S. Customs Service during her junior and senior years in college. Like many political science students, Lisa found that her coursework reinforced her understanding of the federal government, and that her practical work experiences supplemented her classroom learning. But like many young employees, Lisa concluded that working in the federal government had its pros and cons:

> I gained valuable opportunities to work with many people, and to learn their everyday duties and responsibilities. I also made a lot of contacts and gained experiences that would have taken years to grasp on the outside. I really believe that I have a stronger résumé than most of my fellow graduates. On the downside, I found the federal hiring processes inconsistent. If you are waiting for a job vacancy to come up, sometimes it takes months, and sometimes it takes days. It could be the same job but in different offices. This unpredictability is frustrating at times.[3]

Lisa recently graduated and is now pursuing full-time work in both the federal government and private sector.

Working for Congress and Its Members

There are many opportunities for political science students to work in a senator's or representative's Washington or home district office, or on the staff of a congressional committee. A congressional internship or full-time position allows you to work on important policy issues, engage in career networking, and even be a part of history! If you polled the most influential bureaucrats, lobbyists and professional staff in Washington, chances are good that a majority of them got their start by working in a congressional office. Despite Congress' reputation as a bastion of power-hungry and stuffy politicians, the reality is that most of the work done there is by talented and hard-working people in their 20s or 30s.

Legislative internships and full-time staff positions offer excellent entry-level career opportunities for political science majors. House members typically have much smaller staffs and offices (about ten Washington staff on average) than Senators (approximately 25 to 40 staff in Washington).

But you don't have to move to Washington to work for a Congress member or senator since representatives typically have one to three offices in their home districts, and senators have three or more offices spread throughout their home states. Because the culture of legislative careers includes the expectation that you work your way up from an internship, most paid staff members begin as interns or volunteers. Usually an internship (full or part-time) of two or three months is sufficient to position you for a paid job in that or another legislative office.

As with most workplaces, in congressional offices you are expected to start at the bottom and work your way up. Basic staff positions include *staff assistants*, who fulfill miscellaneous duties such as answering phones, greeting visitors, sorting mail, giving tours, supervising interns and supporting more senior staff. *Legislative correspondents* work on answering the numerous letters and requests for information and services from members. Employees in these two entry-level positions usually make in the high $20,000s to low $30,000s per year range. Middle-level congressional positions include *legislative assistants,* who track and develop legislation in several policy areas for their members, and *press secretaries,* who help communicate their members' official positions to media, constituents, and interest groups. Annual salaries for these positions usually fall in the $30,000s to $50,000s range. Finally, *chiefs of staff* or *staff directors* oversee all aspects of the Capitol Hill and district offices, and serve as primary advisors to their members. *Legislative directors* manage all policy aspects of the offices. These senior-level staff make in the $50,000s to over $100,000s range, depending on various factors including their years of experience and whether or not they also do committee work.

Because congressional employees often work long hours for minimal pay, staff turnover is high. This work culture encourages young people to stay a couple of years to gain experience, and then move on to something else. Middle to upper-level staffers are often lured to more lucrative positions in lobbying firms, government agencies, and trade and nonprofit associations. Yet, many people who take jobs in Congress with the expectation of leaving after a year or two end up staying because they find the rewards too great. John Scheilbie, Deputy Chief of Staff to Representative Carrie Meeks (D-Fl), and Associate Staff to the House Appropriations Committee, started as an unpaid intern in 1974 and has worked for several representatives and senators since then. According to Scheilbie: "The federal government is the largest human enterprise on earth. To work in it is a difficult but very satisfying thing. Congress is constantly changing, and I'm learning every single day." [4]

Career Profile: Ben Murphy

While working on his degree in Government and International Politics, Ben Murphy interned for his hometown's congressional representative, Tom Udall (D New Mexico). For two years Ben worked as a paid intern for 20 hours a week during school years, and 40 hours a week during summers. During his internship Ben researched the topic of campaign finance reform, and produced several research papers on the subject for his classes. Ben also became the office "expert" on campaign finance reform who was responsible for monitoring what other Congress members were doing on the subject. According to Ben: "As a congressional staffer I had access to the Library of Congress and the Congressional Research Service, which were really helpful in finding the latest research and data on campaign finance. I also tried to attend every hearing on the subject that I could."[5] Ben's Capitol Hill experience helped him get a paid internship at Travesky & Associates, a consulting firm in Fairfax, Virginia that specializes in transportation policy. Ben is now considering applying for law or graduate school upon graduation.

Federal Intelligence and Law Enforcement Careers

Unfortunately, with the terrorist attacks of September 11, 2001 came a greater need for qualified people in federal intelligence and law enforcement. While high profile agencies such as the Federal Bureau of Investigation (FBI), Central Intelligence Agency (CIA) and Secret Service get a lot of attention from students, there are dozens of other departments and agencies that perform intelligence and law enforcement duties including the Bureau of Alcohol, Tobacco and Firearms, the Fish and Wildlife Service, and the newly-created Department of Homeland Security.

Even though the Office of Personnel Management oversees most federal hiring, specific application procedures among federal law enforcement agencies vary greatly. Some agencies, such as the FBI and CIA, are exempt from OPM's competitive service procedures and instead hire their own employees directly. To apply, you must contact these specific agencies for more information.

Generally, applicants for federal law enforcement and intelligence agencies must be U.S. citizens, hold a four-year degree from an accredited college or university, and pass a rigorous written and physical exam. Applicants with special skills and experiences, including foreign language proficiency in certain languages including Chinese, Arabic and Russian, prior law enforcement or armed forces experience, and advanced technology or quantitative skills are more likely to get hired than applicants without those skills and experiences. Since all applicants who pass the written and physical examinations face a thorough background investigation, a clean police record and lifestyle history are essential.

Pros and Cons Associated with Government Careers

For many people, federal employment offers significant benefits.[6] First, government employees enjoy comparatively good benefits including paid vacation and sick leave, paid holidays, medical insurance, retirement plans and often tuition assistance. In addition, government employees often enjoy greater job security than private-sector workers. While government jobs are not guaranteed, they are more insulated from the normal business cycles and temporary economic setbacks that can result in the loss of private-sector jobs. Perhaps most important, government jobs offer real opportunities to do public service. While public employees are paid livable salaries, the real compensation often lies in the satisfaction of helping people, or making a real impact on public issues.

For others with different personal and work values, government service may have several disadvantages. First, government jobs are usually considered less prestigious than private-sector jobs, even though the job functions are roughly the same. While "prestige" is difficult to measure, it's clear that government workers have attracted a reputation (sometimes deserved, sometimes undeserved) for lacking initiative, drive, and a sense of satisfaction in doing their job well. A second drawback is that many government jobs don't pay as well as similar positions in the private sector. The GS systems' rigidity means that when cost-of-living differences for each region are taken into account, employees in regions with higher costs make less than those in regions with lower costs. And while government workers generally enjoy adequate sick and vacation leave, their health and retirement plans may lag behind those in major corporations or workplaces with strong union representation. Finally, government employees must do without the additional benefits that some private sector employers offer including stock options, employee discounts or Christmas bonuses.

The above points about salary should be taken with a grain of salt. In some education areas, including political science and law enforcement, federal starting salaries are actually close to, if not better than the non-government market averages. According to Howard Risher, some college graduates earn higher average salaries in federal positions than their qualifications would justify in the private sector. In fact, a 1997 study by the Congressional Budget Office showed that some new federal employees with strong work skills are actually paid better than the private-sector market average.[7] Most likely, with demand for government workers rising sharply over the next few years, average salaries will rise, although not always on par with private-sector averages.

Additional Resources

- Through its USAJobs website, the Office of Personnel Management offers a free electronic Career Interest Questionnaire and Interest Guide. Your answers to questions measuring interest in performing specific duties are compiled and your personal work profile is generated. Users can then link broad interests to specific job titles in the federal government. Go to <career.usajobs.opm.gov/explor/guideeq.asp>.

- The Careers in Government website is an extensive and well-organized clearinghouse of information and statistics about jobs in all levels of government. It includes job listings, resume tips, and information about current employment trends. The site also compiles information about internship and other student employment programs for most federal departments and agencies. Found at <www.careersingovernment.com>.

- For a comprehensive web source for student employment opportunities in various government agencies and offices throughout the U.S., visit www.studentjobs.gov. Also go to <studentjobs.gov/agency.htm> for a list of career articles and job descriptions associated with different government, departments, agencies or specific offices.

Specific department and agency web sites include:
- Department of State—Main website, <www.state.gov>. Website for student employment information, <www.state.gov/m/dghr/student>.

- Department of Treasury—Main website, <www.ustreas.gov. Website for student employment information, <www.ustreas.gov/jobs/intern.html>.
- Department of Commerce—Main website, <www.commerce.gov>. Website for student employment information, <ohrm.doc.gov/jobs/Student/default.htm>.

- Department of Health and Human Services--Main website , <www.hhs.gov>. Website for employment opportunities , <www.hhs.gov/jobs/>.

- Department of Housing and Urban Development—Main website, <www.hud.gov>. Website for HUD intern program,

31

<www.hud.gov/offices/adm/jobs/internship/cfm>.

- Department of Interior—Main website, <www.doi.gov>.
  Website for DOI intern programs,
  <www.doi.gov/hrm/employ5.html>.

- Department of Agriculture—Main website, <www.usda.gov>.
  Website for internships and special employment programs,
  <www.usda.gov/da/employ/intern.htm>.

---

[1] As reported in Ellen Nakashima, "Budget to Drop Pay Raise Parity," *Washington Post*, 2-2-02, p. A5.
[2] "The Coming Job Boom," *Time,* 5-6-02, p. 43.
[3] Interview with the author.
[4] Comments made to George Mason University students on Capitol Hill, 7-25-02.
[5] Interview with the author.
[6] The following discussion is derived from Neale Baxter, *Opportunities in Government Careers*, Chicago: VGM Career Books (2001).
[7] "Patriotism and Pay," *GovExec.Com.* 10-8-01. <www.govexec.com/news/>

information, <ohrm.doc.gov/jobs/Student/default.htm>.

- Department of Health and Human Services--Main website ,
  <www.hhs.gov>.
  Website for employment opportunities , <www.hhs.gov/jobs/>.

- Department of Housing and Urban Development—Main website,
  <www.hud.gov>. Website for HUD intern program,
  <www.hud.gov/offices/adm/jobs/internship/cfm>.

- Department of Interior—Main website, <www.doi.gov>.
  Website for DOI intern programs,
  <www.doi.gov/hrm/employ5.html>.

- Department of Agriculture—Main website, <www.usda.gov>.
  Website for internships and special employment programs,
  <www.usda.gov/da/employ/intern.htm>.

---

[1] As reported in Ellen Nakashima, "Budget to Drop Pay Raise Parity,"
Washington Post, 2-2-02, p. A5.
[2] "The Coming Job Boom," *Time,* 5-6-02, p. 43.
[3] Interview with the author.
[4] Comments made to George Mason University students on Capitol Hill,
7-25-02.
[5] Interview with the author.
[6] The following discussion is derived from Neale Baxter, *Opportunities in
Government Careers*, Chicago: VGM Career Books (2001).
[7] "Patriotism and Pay," *GovExec.Com.* 10-8-01.
<www.govexec.com/news/>

4. State and Local Government

Over the last several decades state and local governments have increased their activities in response to a significant rise in the U.S. population and a shift in program funding and responsibility from the national government to state and local jurisdictions. State and local governments currently provide a host of services to residents including education, transportation, utilities, police, courts and probation. There are numerous employment opportunities in the 50 state governments, and approximately 3,000 county governments, 19,400 municipal governments, 16,600 townships, 13,700 school districts, and 34,700 special districts.[1] Because of the great variation among states and regions in the U.S., this chapter can only present an overview of some career opportunities in state and local governments. Students interested in working for government at the state or local level should explore the many opportunities available in their area as well.

The U.S. Department of Labor projects a nearly 12 percent increase in the total number of wage and salary workers in state and local government between 1998 and 2008.[2] Specific sector increases include a projected 21.3 percent increase in social and human service assistants, a 19.5 percent increase in service workers, an 8.4 percent increase in executive, administrative and managerial positions, and a 7.7 percent increase in office and administrative support supervisors and managers. These numbers, however, should be taken with a grain of salt. Since the time these Department of Labor projections were released, most states and local jurisdictions have experienced declining budget revenues that in many cases have slowed new hiring plans or halted them completely. Obviously, the staff and program needs still exist, but many jurisdictions are simply incapable of budgeting for new hires, and in many cases people are being laid off. The implications of these fiscal restraints for current college students will likely be mixed. On the one hand many state and local governments will experience temporary hiring freezes. Yet, on the other many jurisdictions may resort to temporary hiring programs to meet their needs. Such programs may be particularly suited for new graduates who haven't accrued significant work experiences. In addition, while state and local governments are currently experiencing difficulties, the record of past budget crises suggest that things will get better, and that programs will once again expand to catch up with the demand.

Promising career paths in state and local government include the service sector, administrative support, city management, and legislative affairs. The teaching profession, which constitutes a significant proportion of all local and state workers, will be covered in Chapter 13.

Service Professions

Service occupations comprise approximately 31 percent of jobs in state and local government, the largest proportion of all state and local government employees. Positions within the service sector include law enforcement (police and sheriff's officers,) courts personnel (court clerks), correctional officers (jailers, probation officers), social workers, and firefighters.

Police officers work in municipal police departments that vary widely in size. In rural areas with smaller police departments a policy officer may fulfill several duties including crime investigation, traffic enforcement, and response to calls. In larger departments an officer may be assigned to specific units such as traffic enforcement, community policing, gang suppression, narcotics, or special weapons and tactics (SWAT). County law enforcement agencies include sheriffs departments that are primarily responsible for providing security in county jails and courts, but can also perform other law enforcement and investigative tasks. State troopers or highway patrol officers patrol state highways and assist other police jurisdictions in apprehending criminal suspects.

Most law enforcement positions are governed by state or county civil service systems, which screen applicants based on competitive examinations, education records, physical fitness, and personal backgrounds. Before being assigned to full-time duty law, enforcement trainees must complete a basic training program that could last 14 weeks or more.

The availability of employment in state and local law enforcement varies depending on state or local budgets, the pool of eligible retirees, and the needs of local jurisdictions. Jobs in state law enforcement agencies are generally more competitive than those in municipal departments, although the level of competition can vary greatly at the local level. The median annual earnings of police and sheriff's patrol officers were $39,790 in 2000, with the middle 50 percent of officers earning between $30,460 and $50,230 a year.[3] Detectives and criminal investigators earned a median annual income of $48,870. In addition to offering standard benefits including paid vacation, sick leave and retirement, most law enforcement positions offer significant opportunities to accrue overtime hours which can significantly increase an officer's yearly income.

Career Profile: Don Beezley

Don Beezley is a Supervising Probation Officer with the Special Enforcement Unit in the Probation Department of Orange County, California. His primary responsibility is to ensure that adult offenders meet the conditions of their court-imposed probation. Don supervises a team of law enforcement officers that includes two canine teams for conducting drug searches, a computer forensics expert, a methamphetamine search team, and several county officers who also conduct searches.

Don attained his current position after working his way up through county probation over the last 17 years. While working on his undergraduate degree in political science in 1985, Don was hired as a Deputy Probation Counselor at Orange County Juvenile Hall. After a couple of years at Juvenile Hall, he worked as a Deputy Probation Officer with a caseload of juveniles. Don then moved to the county's Gang Violence Suppression Unit for juveniles and adults. From there he was appointed Supervising Probation Officer.

Don cites several positive aspects of his job:

> Our job is half social worker, half cop. In a way we are resource brokers in that people come in with problems and we have a list of services we refer them to. If they don't follow up they go to jail. The main reward is that you get to watch some people who come into the system with a problem actually get better and return to a functional life. Our training is quite good. We receive at least 40 hours of training a year on things like recognizing various forms of abuse, and techniques in 'verbal judo' that help us deescalate people who are agitated. The civil service benefits are also good. I get a steady paycheck, good medical and insurance benefits,

37

and I can retire at age 55 with 95 percent of my salary. [4]

Don suggests that the employment opportunities in county probation departments for political science majors are quite promising. While hiring trends will remain cyclical based on personnel needs and budget constraints, "there are significant entry level opportunities in local or state institutions, like juvenile hall. Once you enter the system and get further training and on-the-job experience, you will be a strong candidate in a number of jurisdictions," explains Don.

Political science students interested in a career in law enforcement or probation should consider taking courses in subjects such as criminal justice, sociology, and public law.

Administrative Sector
Administrative personnel comprise about 21 percent of total state and local government jobs. Administrative professionals provide basic functions in numerous areas including taxation, social services, budgets, elections, and transportation systems (roads, buses, trains and subways). Because taxes and budgeting make up a large part of local governments' responsibilities, financial administrators will remain crucial professionals who collect taxes, prepare budgets, and track expenditures. Tax assessors are also essential positions at the local level since real estate taxes supply a large portion of local revenues.

Political science students interested in pursuing government employment opportunities in administrative support should supplement their core understanding of government and politics with more specialized courses in state and local government, budgeting, accounting, economics, and statistics or quantitative analysis.

City Managers[5]
The council-manager form of government is the most common one among cities with populations over 10,000. One individual, the City Manager (also called *county administrator*, *town manager*, or *chief administrative officer*) oversees the functioning of all government departments. Simply put, managers implement the policies of the elected officials for whom they work. Managers also work with elected officials and citizens to develop future plans for the community in areas like housing, roads and

social services. In many localities city managers are appointed by city councils to manage the various departments of cities and towns.

Most city managers hold a at least a master's degree in public administration, or in a related field such as urban planning. Aspiring managers typically train on-the-job as management analysts or assistants in government departments. The average yearly salary for city managers in 2000 was $75,000, although salaries vary widely among medium-sized and smaller cities. According to Douglas Harman, former City Manager of Fort Worth, Texas:

> Local governments face a wide range of issues and problems, and there is no more gratifying intellectual opportunity than to dissect, analyze and guide them towards solutions. Perhaps even more gratifying than the manager's direct involvement is the opportunity to create a dynamic environment in which persons can deal with these issues creatively and energetically.[6]

To position yourself for a career as a city manager, you should gain significant experience in local government, and consider adding a graduate degree in public administration in the future.

Legislative Assistants
Because all laws governing state and local jurisdictions are passed by city councils, county boards, and state legislatures, many opportunities exist in legislative support positions. State and local legislative bodies perform similar functions as the U.S. Congress including holding hearings, passing budgets, and reviewing or confirming executive appointments. Such positions include legislative aids and analysts, and, legislative committee staff members. As with entry level positions in Congress, students interested in working for local or state legislatures should seriously consider working first as a volunteer or intern. In fact, in many locales unpaid volunteer work or internships are considered a necessary prerequisite for a paid full time position.

Career Profile: Ana Tolentino
For the last two years Ana Tolentino has worked as an Administrative Aide to County Supervisor Gerald Connolly, in Fairfax, Virginia. She

balances this part-time position with her undergraduate studies in Government and International Politics. Ana's duties include advising the supervisor on health and human services issues, working with low income residents to obtain Section 8 housing benefits, and assisting the her boss during county board meetings. Ana finds that working in county government provides real opportunities to help people on a day-to-day basis:

> I like local government because you really have an impact on people. I advocate on behalf of people with problems, and they often write me back and thank me for helping them. Local government is big in terms of what we deal with. Most people don't realize how much is done at the local level, including education and social services. It's the least known of governments, but probably the most important for people's everyday lives. The people I work with like what they do, even the ones who have been doing this for the last 20 or 30 years.[7]

Ana started in county government as an intern, and became so indispensable to her office that they offered her a paid job. Her advice to other students is to "use internships or volunteer opportunities to gain experience and training. I know several people who started at the bottom and are now assistant directors." While Ana is a strong advocate of internships, she realizes that most people have to maintain a paid job to stay in school:

> I've had to pay my way though school, so I understand people have to work. I had to make room for both paid work and my unpaid internship, and that required some serious belt tightening. But it was well worth it because I'm now earning a decent wage in county government. I don't know if I want to do this for the rest of my life, but for now it's a great experience.

Education and Training

Although a political science degree will offer broad knowledge of government and politics, students interested in a career in state or local government should consider taking specific courses in public administration, budgeting, human resource management, economics, and public policy (particularly on issues including transportation, education, social services, health care, and the environment). As with federal workers, state and local employees increasingly utilize complex data management tools and statistical analyses. Thus, to strengthen your resume you should also develop your computer and data analysis skills.

Additional Resources

- State and Local Government on the Net, found at <www.statelocalgov.net>, provides convenient access to a wide variety of links to government information.

- Founded in 1933, the Council of State Governments serves the executive, judicial and legislative branches of state government through leadership education, research and information services. Students can access information on innovative programs and employment opportunities in all state governments. Found at <www.csg.org>.

- The U.S. Conference of Mayors is the official nonpartisan organization of cities with populations of 30,000 or more. Located at <www.usmayors.org>, the Conference website features updates new programs and innovations in U.S. cities.

- The International City/County Management Association, found at <www.icma.org>, provides job descriptions about city managers and related office functions.

- Information about careers in sheriff's departments is provided at the National Sheriff's Association website, at <www.sheriffs.org>.

- The International City/County Management Association , at <www.icma.org>, compiles information on local internship opportunities.

[1] Most of the statistics and job descriptions in this chapter are derived from the Bureau of Labor Statistics' Career Guide, U.S. Department of Labor, at <www.bls.gov/oco/cg.cgs042.htm>.

[2] Department of Labor statistics reported in Neale Baxter, *Opportunities in Government Careers*. Chicago: VGM Career Books (2001).

[3] Earnings statistics provided at <www.collegegrad.com/careers/>.

[4] Interview with the author.

[5] Other chief executives positions in state and local governments include governors, lieutenant governors, and mayors will be discussed in Chapter 12.

[6] Quoted in, *What is the Local Government Management Profession? (2002)*. Report compiled by the International City/County Management Association. Accessed online at <www.icma.org>.

[7] Interview with the author.

5. *International Affairs*

The sub-field of international affairs is one of the most popular among undergraduate students in political science among undergraduates. This is not surprising since the fields of diplomacy, international trade, human rights, democratization and development remain at the forefront of contemporary concerns, while "globalization" has become a catchword to describe the increasing interdependence of peoples and economies in the twenty-first century.

When students first inquire about careers in international affairs, they usually mention international organizations such as the United Nations or World Bank, government departments such as the U.S. State Department, or embassies representing the U.S. or other countries. While these popular choices do offer career possibilities for political science graduates, there are scores of other viable options that get less attention, but for many students may offer better career opportunities.

To begin weighing all your career options, you should first clarify what draws you to international affairs as a potential career field. Are you primarily interested in things like travel, foreign language skills, or in the history and culture of a particular region of the world? If so, you can consider a wide range of options in both the public and private sector. On the other hand, if your interests are more specific, such as diplomacy or international trade, you will need to be more specific in your career search.

The main employment categories for jobs involving international affairs include governments, international non-governmental organizations (NGOs), nonprofit organizations or private volunteer organizations (PVOs), and the private business sector. This chapter provides an overview of these options. Students interested in pursuing careers in international affairs should do more thorough research and talk with as many people as they can about possible opportunities including their professors, career advisors, and actual professionals working in the field.

Federal Government Opportunities in International Affairs
Congress
The federal government offers many options for political science majors interested in international affairs. The U.S. Congress, especially the Senate, has many members and committees that work on international

issues. To gain useful skills and experiences you might consider working in the local or Capitol Hill office of a Congress member who specializes on international issue, or who sits on one of various congressional committees or subcommittees including the Senate Foreign Relations Committee, which handles matters related to national security policy, foreign policy, and international economic policy, or the House International Relations Committee, which handles the same issues on the House side. Other congressional committees that consider matters of international affairs include House Committees on Agriculture, Appropriations, Armed Services, and Energy and Commerce. Other Senate committees that deal with international affairs include Agriculture and Forestry, Appropriations, Armed Forces, and Commerce. All House committee websites can be easily accessed at <www.house.gov>, while Senate committee websites can be found at <www.senate.gov>.

Almost all federal departments and agencies deal with international issues to a greater or lesser extent. Those more heavily involved with international affairs include the U.S Department of State, which conducts all U.S. diplomacy, the Departments of Commerce and Agriculture, which are primarily concerned with U.S trade and overseas development, and the U.S. Agency for International Development (USAID), which sponsors numerous projects around the globe that promote democracy and economic development.

<u>U.S. State Department</u>
The Department of State (DOS) is responsible for formulating and implementing U.S. foreign policy and assisting U.S. citizens abroad. DOS is divided into many bureaus organized along regional (e.g., Bureau of African Affairs) and functional lines (e.g., Bureau for Democracy, Bureau of Economic and Business Affairs). DOS's corps of Foreign Services Officers (FSOs) and Civil Service professionals are involved in various international issues including conflict resolution, human rights, democracy, economic development, environmental law, nuclear non-proliferation, and promotion of America's political and business interests abroad.

Recent developments involving the United States overseas and the anticipated retirement of a large portion of the federal workforce suggest there will be an increasing need for FSOs, although the hiring process remains long and very competitive. There are several stages to the hiring process including a written exam, which interested applicants can register for online at <www.state.gov>, and an oral exam for those who pass the written exam. The remaining few who pass the oral exam must successfully complete an extensive background security check. There is no standard way to study for the Foreign Service exam. But interested students should consider the range and depth of knowledge and the level of skills required to pass. Dale Slaght, a career member of the Foreign Commercial Service offers some advice to students who are considering taking the exam:

> If you are not a strong writer, you should look other than the State Department for a career as an FSO. Although you still might be admitted, inadequate writing skills would likely retard your advancement. For the exam itself, you should have a good grounding in American government and should know American history well. It's also helpful to read the *Washington Post* or the *New York Times* every day. A good magazine like *The Economist* will also give you a broad international focus. With respect to the oral exam, they are not always looking for how much you know, but how well you respond. You need to be forceful and persuasive, not timid. They are looking for assertive people."[1]

The Civil Service offers a second career path in the U.S. State Department. Civil Service positions at State are organized into six functional categories: Operations, Professional and Analytical, IT Engineers and Security, Office Support Professionals, Finance and Accounting, and Executives. Unlike Foreign Service applicants, those seeking Civil Service positions must first identify job vacancies and then apply for them individually. Civil Service employees at State enjoy the same benefits as regular Federal Civil Service employees. For more information, go to <www.careers.state.gov/civil/home.html>.

Career Profile: Maria Pica
Maria Pica is a Senior Advisor to the Assistant Secretary for Democracy, Human Rights and Labor in the U.S. State Department. Ms. Pica advises the Assistant Secretary on several issues including corporate

responsibility, freedom of expression, women's rights, and conflict diamonds. She was a member of the U.S. Delegation to the 56th and 57th U.N. Commissions on Human Rights, where she helped negotiate resolutions on women, children, trafficking, and freedom of expression. Prior to joining the State Department, Ms. Pica gained international policy experience in Congress. She served as Senior Foreign Policy Advisor to Senator Robert Torricelli, and she covered regional economic and humanitarian issues for the Foreign Relations Committee. In the House of Representatives she served as Deputy Counsel to the House Foreign Relations Committee. As a congressional staffer Ms. Pica traveled to North Korea to evaluate U.S. humanitarian donations, and to the Balkans to assess the interim peacekeeping forces.

Ms. Pica received her bachelor's and law degrees from Catholic University in Washington, D.C.[2] Her own career experiences suggest there are various paths to a governmental position in diplomacy:[3]

> If you are not sure where you want to go, keep all your options open and narrow down as you go. I went to law school to get the tools and skills, not to be a litigator. After law school I focused on trade, hoping to get a job in the Department of Commerce. In the meantime, I interned at the Department of Justice, where I worked in the International Division on extradition cases. This was a fantastic opportunity. While still waiting for a Commerce position to open up, a colleague suggested working on Capitol Hill, which I had never even thought of before. After 17 cold calls one person suggested I apply for the Senate International Relations Committee, where I eventually became Deputy Counsel. During a briefing on the Hill I met an Assistant Secretary of State. Two years later he called me and asked if I wanted to work in his Office of Corporate Responsibility. That's how I got into the State Department.

Several student employment and internship programs at State offer excellent opportunities for political science majors. These include the U.S.

Department of State Internship Program, which is open to full or part-time college juniors, seniors, and graduate students. Applicants must be U.S. citizens and in good academic standing at an accredited institution. Domestic internships are located in Washington and some large U.S. cities, while overseas internships are available at embassies and consulates abroad. Interns usually work for one semester or quarter during the academic year, or a minimum of 10 weeks during the summer. For more information on all federal student employment programs, visit <studentjobs.gov/Agency.htm>.

Department of Commerce

Trade exports and imports are of major concern to all developed and developing countries, and to regional trading blocks. Many agencies and offices within the Department of Commerce work on issues of trade and international affairs including the U.S.A Trade Center, the International Trade Administration (ITA), the U.S. Export Assistance Centers (USEAC), the Bureau of Industry and Security, and the Trade Information Center (TIC). Job opportunities at Commerce, including full and part-time positions and student internship programs dealing with international issues, can be found at <www.commerce.gov/jobs.htm>.

Department of Agriculture

The Department of Agriculture also maintains several offices and positions dealing with international issues, including the U.S. Foreign Agriculture Service (FAS), which works to increase the U.S. agricultural exports. The FAS maintains a worldwide network of agricultural counselors, attachés, and trade offices that monitor international markets, compile trade data, and make policy recommendations. Student employment and internship opportunities in the FAS include the USDA Summer Internship Program, located in Washington, DC, and the International Internship Program, among several other programs. Information about the FAS and its employment opportunities can be found at <www.fas.usda.gov/admin/student/>.

U.S. Agency for International Development

The U.S. Agency for International Development (USAID) administers all U.S. foreign aid programs and projects worldwide. Its goals are to advance U.S. foreign policy interests while assisting people around the globe in several functional areas including economic growth, health, and democratization. USAID works with nonprofit organizations, businesses, educational institutions, local governments and indigenous peoples to create and implement programs. There are several full-time and limited-duration employment opportunities at USAID including the New Entry Level Program (NEP), which provides opportunities for qualified applicants to enter USAID's Foreign Service ranks. Foreign Service Professionals are rotated between Washington and overseas assignments of several years' duration. Applicants must be U.S. citizens, and are screened based on education, experience, and skills. For more information, go to <www.usaid.gov/about/employment/nepbro.htm>. USAID also offers several summer internship opportunities for students with U.S. citizenship at its Washington offices and overseas bureaus. Information on internships can be found at <www.usaid.gov/about/employment/intern.htm>.

Many other U.S. Cabinet Departments and Agencies, including the Departments of Energy, Education and Justice, have offices and bureaus that work on international issues. More information is provided on their individual websites.

U.S. Armed Forces
The U.S. military branches (Army, Navy, Air Force, Marines, Coast Guard) offer recruits significant options for advanced training and work experiences that can later be applied to careers in international affairs, along with opportunities for extensive travel. Military personnel learn skills that transfer well to the private sector or to other government jobs, and often can gain tuition assistance or direct opportunities to pursue an advance degree. Prior military service can boost an applicant's chances for employment in government departments and agencies including the Central Intelligence Agency and the State Department. For more information on military careers, and useful links to all the military branches, visit <www.militarycareers.com>.

Peace Corps
Ever since its creation in the mid 1960s, the Peace Corps has sent thousands of college graduates overseas to work in teaching and community development, and on a host of other projects. Peace Corps workers take two-year assignments in a variety of countries. While the pay is not great, the experiences can be very rewarding. In addition, the Peace Corps remains a prestigious program that offers significant opportunities to develop international skills and experiences. Under President Clinton's

urging the federal government began a significant increase in support for Peace Corps programs that continues under the current Bush Administration. One new program, the Peace Corps Masters International Program, offers one year of class work that supplements two years of field work. For more information about all Peace Corps programs, go to <www.peacecorp.gov>.

State and Local Governments and International Affairs
You don't have to move to New York or Washington to gain governmental experience in international affairs. While most attention is focused on the federal government's involvement in international affairs, local and state governments are significant players in globalization as well. They are heavily involved in foreign trade, international tourism, and cultural and educational exchanges, among various other activities.

International trade is among the top agenda items for state and local governments, and millions of dollars are spent each year to promote exports and overseas business development. For example, most states maintain foreign trade offices in large cities abroad to promote export business opportunities. California, for example, maintains nine foreign trade offices in cities including Mexico City, Hong Kong, and Seoul. Professionals who have backgrounds in areas involving international affairs, economics, and international relations staff these offices, along with the state trade and commerce agencies that support them. State trade officials also work out of regional state centers. Minnesota, for example, created the Minnesota Trade Office (MTO) in 1983 to coordinate the state's trade activities. Since then, the MTO has become the hub for trade activities in the three-state region that includes North Dakota and South Dakota. Generally, state trade officials will speak one or more foreign language, and will often have prior experience in state government or international business.

Because the U.S. is a major tourist destination for international visitors, most states and many locales maintain tourism offices that promote their tourist areas overseas. These offices work with other countries and international organizations to attract visitors, and rely on internationally savvy people to help find and maintain working relations with other countries and international organizations.

Increasingly, state legislators are adding specializations in international issues such as border relations, immigration, and trade, and more state legislatures are creating special committees or subcommittees to deal with international issues. Legislative staff positions in members' offices or committees provide great ways to develop your knowledge of international issues, and to gain government work experience that will prove helpful in securing future public or private sector employment.

Finally, colleges and universities sponsor numerous international programs involving educational exchanges, economic development, and research in a variety of areas. To gain international experience, students can participate in study abroad programs sponsored by their school, or work as administrative staff or research assistants on university-sponsored international programs.

International Organizations
<u>United Nations</u>
While the options for careers in international affairs have widened significantly in the last few decades, the United Nations (UN) remains one of the most sought after employers in international affairs. This is due in part to the UN's continued high profile in international issues, and its continued prestige around the globe. There are several employment programs in the UN, and various ways to apply for jobs. But the hiring process remains extremely competitive, even for those seeking unpaid internships. Generally, entry-level positions are filled using a competitive exam, while middle and high-level positions are listed on the UN employment website at <www.jobs.un.org>. The UN National Competitive Examination is given every February, with an application deadline in September.

Each agency within the UN system maintains its own hiring policies, application procedures, and human resources department. The larger UN agencies include the Food and Agriculture Organization, the World Health Organization, the United Nations Development Program, and the United Nations Childrens Fund (UNICEF). A complete list of UN agencies, contact information and websites is available at <www.state.gov/p/io/empl/>. For all applicants, in addition to fluency in English or French, knowledge of Arabic, Chinese, Russian, or Spanish is highly desirable.

Other NGOs and PVOs

Numerous international nongovernmental organizations (NGOs) and private volunteer organizations (PVOs) deal with a variety of issues including development, humanitarian assistance, education, democracy, the environment, and health. Career opportunities are located in these organizations' field offices, or in their headquarters, which are typically located in major cities such as New York, Washington, or Geneva. Examples of potential employers include Amnesty International USA, which is a global nonprofit organization that works on behalf of prisoners of conscience, Sister Cities International, which is a nonprofit organization that helps U.S. communities develop "sister city" linkages with cities throughout the world, and the United Nations Association of the USA, which works to promote U.S. involvement in the UN. Most of these organizations offer internship and other student employment opportunities. Other international nonprofits that are based in the U.S. include International Rescue Committee, Catholic Relief Services, CARE, Oxfam, and the International Committee of the Red Cross.

Bilateral and multilateral organizations promote regional security, development and economic and social issues. These organizations include the Organization of American States (OAS), based in Washington, DC, and Intergovernmental Committee on Migration, based in Geneva. Like most international organizations, the hiring process for bilateral and multilateral organizations is highly competitive, and often favors those with good political connections.

Career Profile: Simonas Girdzijauskas

Simonas Girdzijauskas is currently a Program Assistant with the Joint Baltic American National Committee (JBANC). This nongovernmental association worked to gain admission of the Baltic states (Latvia, Estonia, and Lithuania) into the North Atlantic Treaty Organization (NATO). JBANC also seeks U.S. support to promote stability in Central and East Europe. Simonas applied for the job, which is based in Washington, DC, as a senior undergraduate in Government.

Simonas feels he has gained a lot of practical experience in international affairs at JBANC:

> I really like working at our small office—we only
> have three full-time staff—because I get to play a

51

key role instead of just making coffee. I get to be a part of the action, which has been a great experience and contact builder for me. For example, yesterday I attended a reception along with several current and retired ambassadors. While I felt they were out of my league, they didn't act like they were. They treated me just like everyone else.

Simonas suggests that students interested in international affairs should consider the merits of working at a small organization early in their career:

> I had always heard about the larger international organizations. But I see that the smaller NGOs can also provide opportunities to gain experience doing many things. I write letters and meet with a lot of people on different issues. But I also take out my own trash. A lot of students want to work in international affairs, but actually doing what it takes is different. I realize now that it's important to build credibility in this field before you can even think about moving up to a bigger organization and a position with more authority. The international politics field looks romantic from far away, but doing the small jobs gives you a sense of how it really is. [4]

Consulting Firms and Advocacy Organizations

Consulting firms do much of the work for governmental and nongovernmental programs in international affairs. The World Bank, United Nations, and federal departments and agencies such as the State Department, Department of Commerce, and USAID rely heavily on contactors and consultants. The largest firms maintain offices around the world and deal with almost any imaginable topic. Political science graduates who also have a background in foreign languages, finance, information technology, public administration or management may be strong applicants for consulting firms. Many of the larger consulting firms maintain active recruiting programs, and are likely to participate in college fairs or other recruitment events. Examples of larger international consulting firms include Chemonics International, located in Washington, DC, which provides technical assistance to USAID, and Coopers and Lybrand, located in New York City, which maintains a U.S. staff of 15,000 and an international staff of 45,000.[5]

Private Business Sector

Businesses are among the largest employers of individuals in international affairs. In recent years many U.S. based companies have taken advantage of relaxed trade barriers to expand into overseas markets. These companies and traditional multinational corporations that operate in more than one country at a time continue to rely on internationally savvy people. Businesses employ people who specialize in new product and market development, product and office management, and political risk management. International business includes traditional sectors such as banks, oil and chemicals, manufacturers, importers and exporters. Possible employment opportunities include: (1) working for a U.S. based firm seeking clients and business opportunities in other countries; (2) working for an international firm outside the U.S.; and (3) working for a U.S. subsidiary located outside the U.S.

Most international business opportunities are reserved for those who have accumulated significant international experiences in other public sector or nongovernmental organizations, or those who have worked their way up through the ranks of a particular company. If your heart is set on securing an entry-level position in international business, Ron and Caryl Krannich, recognized experts in international careers, suggest your best chances lie with a particular type of business:

> An ideal company providing international travel opportunities would be one just starting to develop overseas operations. During their initial stage of developing new markets and establishing local bases of operations into new countries, numerous opportunities should be available for working abroad...Consequently, your best opportunities in international business may be with small companies just starting to enter the international business arena or expanding into new locations.[6]

Additional Resources

- *Directory of International Internships*, Charles Gliozzo and Vernicka Tyson, eds. Michigan State University Career Services and Placement. www.msu.edu. Updated yearly.

- *International Jobs* (5th ed.), Eric Kocher and Nina Segal. Cambridge: Perseus Books (1999).

- The State Department also maintains a list of current job opportunities and opening among international organizations, including the UN, at <www.state.gov/p/io/empl>.

---

[1] Public comments to students at George Mason University, 11-14-02.
[2] Biographical information provided by U.S. State Department.
[3] Comments made at a State Department briefing for University of California, Santa Barbara interns, 7-26-02.
[4] Interview with the author.
[5] These and other consulting organizations are profiled in Ronald L. Krannich and Carly R. Krannich, *Jobs for People Who Love Travel* (2nd ed.). Manassas Park: Impact Publications (1995).
[6] *Jobs for People Who Love to Travel,* p. 244.

6. Nonprofit Organizations

Like government careers, the nonprofit sector is an expanding field with excellent entry-level career opportunities for recent political science graduates. According to Patricia Lewis, Nonprofit Specialist in Residence at George Mason University, "the nonprofit sector is undergoing explosive growth, and opportunities abound as there currently are not enough qualified people to fill all the jobs. The job market is especially good for people with strong strategic and critical thinking skills." [1] Nonprofits offer great opportunities for people who like to help others, or who believe strongly in certain issues or causes. Unlike government jobs, nonprofits in general offer more flexible employment options for students or recent graduates.

There are many myths about the nonprofit career sector that may discourage students from seriously considering this field. One common misnomer is that nonprofit organizations only employ people who work for no pay. Another mistaken belief is that nonprofits provide their services for free. These beliefs are obviously inaccurate, and distort the reputation of an honorable and potentially rewarding career field. While many nonprofits do welcome volunteers, most also employ professionals who earn competitive salaries. And while some nonprofits are charities, such as the Salvation Army or Red Cross, many, like the YMCA, require fees for their services. Other nonprofits raise funds through donations from individuals, corporations, and charitable foundations.

What are Nonprofits?
Nonprofit organizations promote causes or provide public services in numerous areas including the environment, social services, arts and culture, economic development and science-based research. Nonprofits are different than private corporations or businesses that sell products or provide services to generate profits for their owners or shareholders. Instead, nonprofits are funded through grants from governments, private sector corporations, philanthropic foundations, wealthy individuals, membership dues, and various other fundraising activities. Nonprofits that hold 501 (c) (3) designations from the Internal Revenue Service (IRS) are limited in the government lobbying activities they can pursue, while those holding 501 (c) (4) designations can lobby extensively.

Currently, there are over one million nonprofit organizations in the U.S. that collectively employ over ten million people.[2] There are thousands of other nonprofits, called nongovernmental organizations (NGOs), operating around the globe. Nongovernmental organizations respond to natural disasters such as floods or famine, provide basic services in war-torn areas, and promote rights such as free speech or self-determination, among many other things.

Specific types of nonprofits[3] include *foundations*, which are nonprofits that operate from their own funds and are managed by a board of trustees or directors. Foundations often provide grant support to educational, charitable, cultural and religious organizations. Major foundations include the Carnegie Corporation, Ford Foundation, Kellogg Foundation, Kettering Foundation, Pew Charitable Trust, Sloan Foundation, and the Twentieth Century Fund.

Another type of nonprofit, *advocacy organizations*, promote the interests of those they serve, such as children, the poor, the elderly, or veterans. Examples include Childhelp USA and the Paralyzed Veterans of America. Other nonprofits advocate for a particular public issue such as the environment or human rights. Examples include the Sierra Club or Amnesty International.

Research institutes, also known as *think tanks*, conduct research, produce reports, and organize conferences on a host of public and private-sector topics including economic trends, environmental policy, management effectiveness, foreign affairs, and government reform. Think tanks are usually designated nonprofit organizations that receive funding through grants and contracts from governments, corporations and foundations. Most consider themselves nonpartisan, although many promote liberal or conservative approaches to public problems. The Heritage Foundation, for example, is recognized as a conservative think tank, while the Progressive Policy Institute adopts a more liberal perspective. Other prominent think tanks include the Brookings Institution, the CATO Institute, the Hoover Institute, RAND, and the Woodrow Wilson Center. Most think tanks will employ undergraduate students as interns for a semester or two. Students who intern at think tanks gain valuable research experience as they generally support the work of one or a few scholars. Experience at a think tank may also help undergraduates decide if graduate school is a right choice for them.

Nonprofits vary widely in their size and mission. Large organizations, such as the American Red Cross or YWCA, employ thousands of individuals while the smallest organizations may have one paid employee who oversees a staff of volunteers. Nonprofits offer career opportunities for people who live in the smallest towns to the largest cities. While a list of large nonprofit organizations is provided at the end of this chapter, students who are interested in learning more about nonprofits should not neglect smaller organizations that may operate locally.

Career Profile: Linda Blauhut

Linda Blauhut is Assistant General Counsel for the Paralyzed Veterans of America (PVA). She completed her bachelor's degree at Michigan State University and her law degree at George Washington University. Prior to going to law school, Linda worked at Youth for Understanding, an international exchange program. While in college, she completed several internship programs including the Dow Jones Newspaper Fund Internship and the Sears Congressional Internship Program. Linda joined PVA shortly after graduating from law school. As a nonprofit membership organization, PVA works to maintain Department of Veterans Affairs (VA) health care and research funding for those with spinal cord injuries or diseases. PVA also monitors public and private sector compliance with the Americans with Disabilities Act. According to Linda:

> Our chapters or members may notice things
> involving access to public buildings, and we lobby
> or go to court if necessary to get people to comply
> with the Americans with Disabilities Act. PVA
> also works on behalf of individual veterans,
> helping them secure benefits through filing claims
> with VA or going to court when needed.[4]

Linda offers some advice for students who are considering law school, but who are not sure whether they want to pursue a career in the nonprofit sector:

> Follow the issues you are interested in. Law
> school is what you make of it. It's like a train.

Everyone is going in the same direction, toward a law degree, but if you want to get something more than the basic ride out of it, you have to go to the café car and get it yourself. There is a lot of room in law school for just about everyone. If your primary drive is to make a lot of money, you may go one way. But there are opportunities for people who want to do other things too. However, if you are not sure what you want to do, keep in mind that law school is a lot of work and not the place to 'find yourself.' There is no shame in waiting a few years to see if you are interested in other things. Those who say, 'What the heck, I don't have anything else going right now,' probably shouldn't go to law school.

Issues Versus Skills in the Nonprofit Universe

The dizzying range of size and types of nonprofit organizations can seem overwhelming to college students who are seriously considering a career in nonprofits. Therefore, it's helpful to find ways to narrow down your search for opportunities in either paid positions or in internships or voluntary work.

The basic distinction between issues and skills, first discussed in Chapter 2, offers one way to organize your exploration of nonprofit careers. The nonprofit sector includes many people who are driven by a particular issue they feel strongly about, and who are less concerned about which particular position they fill at a given time. If you are driven primarily by an interest in an issue such as the environment, women's rights, child health, or arts advocacy, you should learn as much as you can about organizations that promote specific variants of those issues. Be sure to consider your options at different levels including international, national, state and locally based nonprofits. Many nonprofits, such as World Wildlife Federation and the American Cancer Society have headquarters that coordinate the work of regional and local chapters, and that engage in political advocacy and fundraising, as well as many regional or local chapters that provide hands-on work that cause-oriented individuals will find fulfilling.

Another approach is to develop skills that are transportable between nonprofits with widely different missions. In larger organizations, and many smaller ones too, there are several essential positions including *fundraisers*, *accountants*, *researchers*, *administrative assistants*, and *communications specialists*. For example, the nonprofit sector is under greater scrutiny from governments, philanthropists, foundations and the general public. In response they must keep more detailed records and reports on what they do and how they do it. They must also constantly work to articulate what they do to various audiences. This creates a greater need for communications and public relations specialists who engage in media relations, web design, publishing, and governmental relations. In addition, there is keen competition among nonprofits to raise funds in order to keep their projects going. Thus, fundraising is a highly desirable skill that is transportable among various nonprofit organizations. The professionals who staff these positions are often not directly involved in promoting the organization's cause or issue, although many are, especially in smaller organizations.

A final approach to narrow your exploration of nonprofits as a possible career is to apply what your know about yourself using the self-assessments in Chapter 2 of this book. If you are an independent-minded person who likes to work outdoors, perhaps a field position in smaller environmental organization will be more suited to you than a staff position in the national headquarters of large advocacy group. If you want to promote a cause, but prefer to work in a corporate setting, a fundraising position in a large nonprofit might be a good choice.

Career Profile: Edward Villacorta
While completing his degree in political science, Edward Villacorta worked part-time in both the for-profit and nonprofit sectors, and he sees some important differences between the two. Last summer, he worked at the World Wildlife Federation's (WWF) accounting office. According to Edward:

> I liked the office environment a lot. There was a
> positive and friendly attitude among all the staff,
> and a strong 'were all in this together' feeling. I
> found I did better and had more fun doing
> something I was interested in and passionate
> about. This was different from my other jobs in

customer service. In those jobs there seemed to be more backstabbing, and a lot of people pointing fingers at each other saying 'why don't I get what he got?'

Edward's experience with WWF has heightened his interest in the nonprofit field in general, while his coursework has raised his awareness of civil rights as an issue, which he plans to pursue once he graduates:

> In choosing my government classes I began to focus more on issues of civil rights and liberties, and organizations like the American Civil Liberties Union kept coming up. To follow my interests I also added a minor in legal studies, which I hope will help me one day when I apply to law school. But for now I want to work a couple of years before even thinking about law school.[5]

Monetary and "Other" Rewards in the Nonprofit Sector

The conventional wisdom says that nonprofit jobs pay less than private sector and government jobs, especially at the entry level. The traditional thinking is that people who thrive in the nonprofit sector are motivated more by their personal convictions than the profit motive. While it's true that you won't become a millionaire through a career working in nonprofits, the salary picture is generally better than the conventional wisdom assumes. In many cases nonprofit salaries are quite competitive with government and private sector salary scales, especially as you move up into mid-career positions that require higher-level skills and more responsibility, or if you work in larger nonprofits with more institutionalized hiring and promotion practices.

Volunteerism is highly valued in the nonprofit sector. Thus, as with most career sectors internships and other student employment programs can provide invaluable resume-building experiences. The larger nonprofits usually offer internship opportunities in a variety of domestic and international offices, and various units within the organization. Although larger organizations are valid choices, be sure to explore the middle sized and smaller organizations too. Because these organizations operate with less staff and smaller budgets, they often rely heavily on their interns and volunteers to stay running and meet their mission goals. In many cases you are more likely to gain challenging projects and be treated as a regular member of the staff. According to Kristin Watkins of Wider Opportunities, a nonprofit devoted to expanding employment opportunities for low income women, "the benefit of working in a smaller organization is the real sense you gain that your work is meaningful and rewarding, and that if you aren't doing it, it won't get done." [6]

Top U.S. Based Nonprofit Organizations[7]

The following list of large nonprofit organizations is only a sample of the thousands of opportunities in the field.

Salvation Army. Based in Alexandria, VA, the Salvation Army provides the poor and needy with food and shelter services. For more information, go to <www.salvationarmy.org>.

American Red Cross. Based in Washington, D.C., the American Red Cross is the leading relief agency for natural disasters, <www.redcross.org>.

American Cancer Society. Based in Atlanta, GA, the American Cancer Society raises funds for cancer education and research, <www.cancer.org>.

YMCA of the USA. Based in Chicago, IL, the YMCA is the largest community service organization in the U.S., <www.ymca.net>.

YWCA. Based in New York City, the YWCA is the oldest women's membership organization in the U.S. The YWCA's goals are to empower women and eliminate racism. YWCA organizations operate in 101 countries, <www.ywca.org>.

Corporation for Public Broadcasting. Based in Washington, D.C., the Corporation for Public Broadcasting (CPB) was created by Congress in 1967. CPB promotes non-commercial public telecommunications services using television, radio, online and digital formats. Services include financial support to over 1000 public television and radio stations through grants and educational and programming support, <www.cpb.org>.

Additional Resources

- For a searchable list of internships in the nonprofit sector, visit the website of The National Association of Schools of Public Affairs and Administration, at <www.naspaa.org/publicservicecareers/menu.htm>.

- Idealist maintains an extensive list of web resources for people considering careers in the nonprofit sector. Go to <www.idealist.org> for great articles about working in nonprofits, salary and employment trends, and personal profiles of people in various stages of their nonprofit careers.

- Council on Foundations is an organization of grant making foundations and corporations, at <www.cof.org>.

- *100 Best Non-Profits to Work For*, Leslie Hamilton and Robert Trugert. Arco Publishing, (1998).

- *Nonprofits' and Education Job Finder*, Daniel Lauber. Planning Communications, (1997-2000).

- *100 Jobs in Social Change*, Harley Jebens. Macmillan, (1996).

---

[1] Interview with the author.

[2] These and related statistics found at <www.idealist.org/firstjob.html>.

[3] Some nonprofit categories and descriptions are derived from *International Careers: Summaries of the Field*. APSIA Career Services Officers (1998), <www.ksg.harvard.edu/career/apsia/>.

[4] Interview with the author.

[5] Interview with the author.

[6] Comments made at "Getting the Most Out of Your Internship" career panel, George Mason University, (1996).

[7] Information provided at <www.careers-in-markteing.com/nptop.htm>.

7. Law

Like international affairs, law is among the most popular sub-fields among political science students. Law provides a fundamental structure of rules and sanctions without which society cannot function. In the U.S. and other countries with governments based on popular consent, the law regulates the actions of officials and citizens alike. Lawyers and judges are the core functions in the American legal system, but there are numerous other positions and institutions that are integral to our system of law as well. Thus, the career options in law are numerous and varied. This chapter will provide a brief overview of law as a career field, and discuss several important legal positions including lawyers, judges, paralegals, and conflict resolution professionals.

Lawyers
Because the legal system is an integral part of our society, lawyers[1] will always be needed to help individuals, groups, government agencies, and public and private organizations maneuver through the complex and ever-changing legal system. Many lawyers, also known as *attorneys*, work as advocates and advisors to parties in civil and criminal cases. The criminal justice system relies on lawyers to serve as private counsel hired by criminal defendants, as court-appointed counselors to represent indigent criminal defendants, and as prosecutors representing the local or state jurisdiction prosecuting a case. *Criminal lawyers* are responsible for knowing the relevant points of criminal law, explaining those points to their clients or supervisors, and making recommendations about courses of action their clients should take.

While some lawyers accrue many hours in court, most spend the majority of their time outside of court conducting research, interviewing witnesses, preparing for trial, and negotiating with other lawyers and prosecutors. Attorneys who specialize in trial work must be particularly articulate, nimble-minded, and adept at exploiting courtroom rules and procedures for their client's benefit.

Civil lawyers represent parties who are in dispute under civil law. Their main activities include assisting clients in litigation and preparing contracts, wills and trusts. Civil lawyers often specialize in one or more legal areas including taxes, environment, bankruptcy, or intellectual

63

property. Like criminal defense lawyers, civil lawyers can practice singly or as a member of a small, medium, or large law firm.

Contract lawyers provide services in research, legal filings, and trial work for an hourly or contract fee to solo and small firms. This arrangement may be particularly good for law students or recent graduates who need to gain work experience. Firms may also benefit from using contractors as a cost-savings device, or as a way to try our prospective hires without making a full commitment to them up front.

Although the majority of lawyers practice privately, many are employed by a single client such as a for-profit company or corporation, or work for a public entity such as a government agency or nonprofit organization. Some lawyers who are employed by a single client also maintain private practices on the side.

Career Profile: Brian Reznick

While attending the University of California, Santa Barbara, Brian Reznick developed a strong desire to become a lawyer. Even though his ultimate interest was the prosecution side of criminal law, Brian jumped at the chance to work as a summer intern in the Maryland Public Defender's Office. Prior to starting his internship he completed a weeklong training program for interns in his office. According to Brian, "the training was excellent. But I still felt nervous the first time I went out into the field."[2] Brian soon became more comfortable with the position: "Because there was so much work to do in my office, I got to assist lawyers in their investigations by tracking down and interviewing witnesses, serving subpoenas, and helping to prepare statements." Brian also gained helpful skills that will serve him well in the future, including his ability to communicate with people from all walks of life:

> I found my interview skills got better as I went. It helped to have a partner who taught me certain things, like the importance of body language and how to present myself to people. For example, I learned not to cross my arms because many people think you don't believe what they're saying. It's never easy interviewing people about crimes, especially victims. So it was good to work with nine or ten different lawyers, because each had his

or her own style. I tried to absorb the best habits from each of them.

Brian's internship experience exposed him to the work of public defenders and prosecutors, and the more he observed the more convinced he became that the public defender side was better for him:

> In terms of the big cases, prosecutors have the better job. But I found that most of the everyday cases that prosecutors try are drug cases. I wouldn't be comfortable with that for very long. On the public defender's side you are standing up for people. Although the money and prestige may not be as great, you can gain a lot of satisfaction in the important public service you provide.

Brian intends to apply to law school after completing his bachelor's degree.

Formal Training for Lawyers

Political Science ranks among the top majors chosen by students interested in pursuing a career in law. Each year thousands of graduates armed with political science degrees enter law school. Political science classes that can help prepare students for law school include public law, constitutional law, civil rights and liberties, administrative law, and comparative legal systems.

To thrive in a law career you must be able to read critically and think logically, communicate well orally and in writing, and work well with people from all backgrounds. While many students who graduate law school and ultimately pass their Bar Exam will practice law as private attorneys, prosecutors and public defenders, others will work in positions that don't require a law degree but may recognize the degree as a positive part of an employee's resume.

All state and local jurisdictions require that persons who practice law first be admitted to the bar recognized in that region. Admission to the bar requires passing a written bar examination, and in many jurisdictions a separate ethics examination. In most states applicants to the bar must first obtain a bachelor's degree and graduate from an accredited law school. Accreditation can be granted from the American Bar Association or a state association.

Training for the bar typically requires three years of law school beyond the four-year bachelor's degree. Students usually take core law courses in their first year including constitutional law, contracts, property law, and torts, and may choose to specialize in one or more fields of law in their remaining courses. Law schools often employ learning activities such as moot courts, and encourage their best students to submit legal research articles to the school's law journal.

A growing number of part-time night or weekend programs now compete with the traditional full-time law program. These alternative program formats usually take longer than the traditional three-year programs.

Applying to Law School

Many more students apply to law schools than can be admitted. Competition for the best full or part time law programs is intense, with admission to the top programs reserved for only the strongest applicants. In reviewing law school applications, admissions consider several things including an applicant's score on the Law School Admissions Test (LSAT), their cumulative GPA and grades in specific courses, their undergraduate school's national ranking, their letters of recommendation and statement of purpose, and sometimes their work experiences and extra-curricular activities. Marty Carcieri, a former practicing lawyer and consultant to Kaplan who is now an assistant professor of public law at the University of Tennessee, Knoxville, urges prospective law students to be realistic about their qualifications and careful in assessing where they fall in the pool of all law school applicants. According to Professor Carcieri:

> For the top one-third of schools, applicants are
> quickly separated into three piles: (1) automatic
> admits, (2) automatic rejects, and (3) middle range
> possible admits. It is in this third category where
> your letters of recommendation and personal
> statement can make a difference. Basically
> admissions officers look at the quality of your
> references and the type of case you make for your
> self. So it's very important to get to know your

professors well, so that they know you well enough to write you strong letters of recommendation. It is also essential to have a clear sense of why you want to pursue a law degree. If you are unsure about this, admissions officers will sense it and they may pass you over for someone with clearer goals.[3]

Career Outlook for Lawyers

Lawyers were employed in approximately 681,000 legal jobs in 2000, with three out of four practicing privately, and one fourth holding positions in government or other public and private entities. The number of lawyers has grown in proportion to the overall population in the last decades, according to the American Bar Association. For example, the ratio of the general population to attorneys was 691 people for every one attorney in 1950 (691:1). In 1980 the ratio dropped to 418:1, and in 2000 it dropped to 218:1.[4] One might ask: what do all these lawyers do? As mentioned, the increased litigious and regulatory nature of society requires a steady cadre of lawyers. In addition, labor analysts predict a continuing demand for lawyers due to the growth in the population and continuing robust business activity. Finally, lawyers are increasingly necessary to help individuals and groups maneuver through the complex civil law associated with the environment, health care, civil rights, and globalization.

Lawyers' salaries fall in the upper range of most professions. According to the National Association for Law Placement (NALP), the 2000 median salaries of lawyers six months after graduation was $51,900, with new lawyers in private practice averaging $80,000 a year. And according to NALP's 2001 salary survey, the median annual salaries for law associates at private firms ranged from $65,000 for first-year associates to $175,000 for associates in their eight year. The average annual salary of all lawyers working for business or industry was $60,000 a year, and $34,000 a year for those working as public interest.[5]

Paralegals

Individual lawyers, law firms, and other public and private entities employ paralegals to help with administrative and basic legal tasks. *Paralegals* perform many of the same functions as practicing attorneys, but are not admitted to the bar. Increasingly, paralegals are completing tasks traditionally handled by lawyers including preparing witnesses for testimony, researching legal points in cases, drafting pleadings and motions, obtaining affidavits, and helping attorneys during trials. Besides law firms, major employers include the federal government (especially the U.S. Departments of Justice, Treasury and Defense), state and local governments, banks, real estate agencies and insurance companies.

In addition to receiving training through an accredited two or four-year paralegal program, graduates with a bachelor's degree can obtain a paralegal certificate in programs that range from a few months to two years in duration. Many paralegals train on the job in a law firm or other organization, and some can obtain tuition support for outside paralegal training from their existing employer.

The job outlook for paralegals is positive largely because they will continue to provide cheaper alternatives to attorneys in handling routine legal tasks. Earnings for paralegals and legal assistants vary greatly depending on a person's education level, training and experience. The median annual earnings for paralegals in 2000 was $33,360, with the top 10 percent earning over $56,000 and the bottom 10 percent earning less than $23,350. Average yearly earnings for paralegals in the federal government was $48,560, compared to state governments where average earnings were $32,680, and local governments where average earnings were $34,120.[6]

Students who want to work in the legal field, but don't necessarily want to practice law as attorneys should weigh the costs of law school against the average salaries of workers in various legal positions. In some cases adding a law degree to your resume will be a significant boost to your career prospects; in other cases it won't.

Mediators, Arbitrators and Judges

Mediation is a process that attempts to bring parties in a dispute to some resolution without resorting to further legal action and court processes. A *mediator* is a third party who may have formal training in conflict resolution beyond the four-year bachelor's degree. Mediators who practice in state or court-sanctioned mediation programs often must meet training and experience standards for that jurisdiction. Such standards vary widely among different states. Mediators may choose to specialize in one or more areas including business, management, real estate, and family issues.

Arbitration also takes place outside of the formal court system, but the process results in a legally binding decision that is enforceable by the courts. *Arbitrators* are often attorneys or retired judges who work on a fee or limited contract basis. Parties in disputes may choose arbitration to avoid formal court proceedings, but still retain a legal framework that is often more legally binding than agreements reached through mediation.

Mediators, arbitrators, and those who hold similar titles such as *facilitators* or *conflict resolution* specialists can look forward to growing employment opportunities in the future as more people and organizations try to avoid costly litigation in resolving their disputes. Incomes vary widely in these occupations according to the location of the employer and nature of the work.

Judges preside over cases of all types. Their goals are to ensure that trials and hearings are conducted fairly and in accordance with established court procedures and state or federal laws. Judges rule on issues of evidence, witness testimony, and disputes between lawyers on opposing sides of legal disputes or criminal cases. In general, judgeships are among the most prestigious positions in the field of law.

Federal and state judges must usually be lawyers, although many states allow non-lawyers to work as judges in limited areas. Jurisdictions also vary widely in how they select their judges. Some elect their judges, others appoint them, and still others require appointed judges to eventually stand before the voters in retention elections.

The demand for judges will remain strong in the coming decades because of continuing public concern for crime and the increasing number of legal disputes in the private and public sectors. However, many state and local jurisdictions will be unable to meet their hiring needs because of budget constraints. Therefore, job growth will be much more limited for judges as compared to arbitrators and mediators. Because of the high prestige of judgeships, and the equally high pay for judges in many jurisdictions ($78,000 a year average for all judges and magistrate judges[7]), there will never be a shortage of people willing and able to accept the opportunity to serve as a judge.

Additional Resources

- The American Bar Association provides information on careers in law and legal training, at <www.abanet.org>.

- The Law School Admissions Council is a resource for information about the LSAT, law school admissions, and financial aid for law students. Go to <www.lsac.org>.

- The National Association of Legal Assistants is found at <www.nala.org>.

- The National Federation of Paralegal Associations is found at <www.paralegals.org>.

- The American Arbitration Association is found at <www.adr.org>.

- *Career Opportunities in Law and the Legal Industry*, Susan Echaore-McDavid. New York: Facts on File, Inc. (2001).

- *Official Guide to ABA-Approved Law Schools*. Law School Admissions Council and the American Bar Association. Newtown, PA, (2003).

---

[1] Much of the descriptive information in this section is derived from the *Occupational Outlook Handbook*, U.S Department of Labor (2000).

[2] Interview with the author.

[3] Interview with the author.

[4] As reported in Gary Munneke, *Opportunities in Law Careers*. Chicago: VGM Career Books (2001).

[5] National Association for Law Placement statistics as reported in the *Occupational Outlook Handbook* (2000), and in Susan Echaore-McDavid, *Career Opportunities in Law and the Legal Industry*. New York: Facts on File, Inc. (2001).

[6] *Occupational Outlook Handbook* (2000).

[7] 2000 National Occupation Employment and Wage Estimates, U.S. Bureau of Labor Statistics, accessed at <www.bls.gov/oes/2000/oes_23Le.htm>.

8. Lobbying and Interest Advocacy

If you are a "people person" who loves to discuss politics and public policy, you might consider one of the many professional positions within the broad field of interest group advocacy. Interest advocacy encompasses traditional lobbying and related positions in governmental affairs, public relations, and media relations. Organized interests of all shapes and sizes in the U.S. and abroad will continue to need energetic recent graduates, upward climbing professionals, and seasoned careerists. Since there is no slowdown of interest group advocacy in general, there will continue to be significant employment opportunities in this career field.

To weigh the pros and cons of the many career options in interest advocacy, it's helpful to briefly review the history of interest advocacy in the United States.

A Brief History of Organized Interests and Their Activities
Throughout American history organized interests sought to promote their agendas by petitioning government. The practice of interest group advocacy was common when James Madison wrote *The Federalist* #10 in 1788. In this classic statement on the dangers of "faction" in governments based on popular consent, Madison dismisses the notion that society should stifle organized interests or restrict their activities altogether. Instead, we should mitigate factions' potential harm by encouraging the formation of all types of groups. As Madison said: "Extend the sphere [of factions], and you take in a greater variety of parties and interests; you make it less probable that a majority of the whole will have a common motive to invade the rights of other citizens."

The notion that American politics is controlled by special interests that wield too much power is a recurring theme in American history. While some interests do wield disproportionate power and influence in America, the reality is that one person's "special interest" is a vital and necessary interest to another. And since the rights to exercise free speech, to peaceably assemble, and to petition the government for redress of grievances are protected under the Constitution, organized interests will continue to vie for political influence in America whether we like it or not.

The term "lobbyist" comes from the nineteenth century practice where individuals working on behalf of interests such as railroads, banks, farmers and labor unions would line the hallways of legislatures and executive departments at the national, state and local level to press policy makers to promote their interests. In those days, "booze and bribery" were acceptable tactics to win favor with legislators and other government officials. Beginning in the late nineteenth century the practice of lobbying was subject to periodic reforms. Even though most interest group activities today meet existing ethical standards, the public perception of interest groups is still tainted by the residue of past unethical practices.

In recent decades America has experienced a virtual explosion of interest group activity that hasn't slowed. Changes including the civil rights and environmental movements as well as governmental efforts on behalf of women, racial minorities, the disabled, the elderly, the poor, children, and endangered animal species have brought about more organized activity. There has also been significant growth in the number and activities of professional organizations representing individuals in particular professions including trial lawyers, pipe fitters, beer wholesalers and small printers.

There are several types of groups that offer significant employment opportunities for lobbyists and related interest advocacy professionals:

Umbrella Organizations, also called *associations*, represent one segment of society but often take stands on a variety of policy matters that affect their members. These groups include the National Association of Manufacturers, the National Association of Beer Wholesalers, the Trial Lawyers Association, and the AFL-CIO.

Single-Issue Groups organize around a single issue and often attract very committed members who advocate on behalf of that issue. Examples include the National Right to Life Committee, the National Abortion and Reproductive Rights League, and the National Rifle Association.

Public Interest Groups generally speak for broader interests including consumers, children, and environmentalists. Examples include the Sierra Club and the National Taxpayers Union.

Non-Member Groups include corporations that may maintain a lobbying presence in Washington and some state capitals, and private colleges and universities.

State and local governments seek to influence national policymakers directly, or advance their interests through participation in organizations such as the National League of Cities, the U.S. Conference of Mayors, the National Governors Association, and the Council of State Governments.

The last few decades have also witnessed an increase in organized efforts among existing interest groups. More groups employ *lobbyists*, also known as *public affairs* or *government specialists*, than ever before. Lobbyists may be employed "in house" as direct employees of the interest or organization, or as staff of a lobbying firm that advocates on behalf of several organizations.

You don't have to move to Washington to develop the skills and experiences necessary for a career in interest advocacy. Since organized interests operate at the national, state and local level, opportunities for employment are found in various shapes, sizes and places. National organizations including the National Rifle Organization, Sierra Club, National Association of Retired Persons, and the AFL/CIO maintain regional and local operations as well as national headquarters. These organizations lobby the Congress, state legislatures, executive departments and agencies at all levels, and even local county boards or city councils.

Career Profile: Nick Warner

Nick Warner is founder of Nick Warner & Associates, a Sacramento, California lobbying firm that represents law enforcement interests including probation, parole and sheriffs departments before the California State Legislature. Nick earned a bachelor's degree in political science from University of California, Davis, and a Master's degree in Public Administration from Golden Gate University. Prior to founding his lobbying firm, Nick worked as a legal aid for a nonprofit organization, and as a lobbyist for an association representing county supervisors. According to Nick, lobbying is like a "human chess match," where

> you may be working for a client on an issue where
> you need five votes in legislative committee, but
> three members say they won't budge. It's your job
> to find the political pressure points to get their
> attention. You have to constantly think up creative

strategies in your head. You wake up at 3am and think, 'I've got the angle!'[1]

Nick's days are a mixture of public relations, public policy, and raw politics. In reality, however, there isn't one typical day, according to Nick: "One day I'm working the appropriations committee, the next day I'm updating 300 association members, and the next I'm working on media strategy."

Nick offers some advice for political science students who are considering a career in interest advocacy:

> People ask me all the time: 'How can I get a job like yours?' And I ask them: 'What do you bring to the table?' To do well in this field you have to concentrate on substance, not just be a schmoozer. You need to bring an ability to be a strong researcher, and an understanding of political institutions. It also helps to be a policy expert on a particular subject, and have good contacts in that area. Towards that end, you should get active in parties, elections, and government. You should also try to hitch your wagon to the right people who can teach you.

Lobbying as a Profession

Today most middle to large-sized groups employ full time government affairs specialists, or lobbyists, whose purpose is to represent their group's interests before policymakers. Lobbyists try to influence the content of legislation and government regulations, and advocate specific interpretations of existing laws, rules and regulations. Many organizations will also resort to judicial strategies when necessary. An organization's typical government affairs office will include lower to middle-level researchers or information specialists, and higher level associates and directors.

Because they operate in a highly political environment that necessitates compromise, lobbyists must temper their goals to get what is attainable in the short run, while also positioning their organization to push for other policy changes in the long run. Lobbyists can't be everywhere and do everything. Thus, to be effective they must be very strategic in their efforts by focusing on decision makers who may already be predisposed towards their general position, and those who may not agree with their position but are not hostile to it either. Likewise, legislators and other policymakers cannot know everything on every issue. They must rely on others including personal staff, other policy makers, party leaders, and even interest group representatives to provide cues on what position to take. Thus, to be effective lobbyists must present reliable information about their organization's position, and the positions of those they oppose. If a lobbyist gains a reputation for shading the truth, he or she will quickly lose credibility among policymakers.

Many interest group advocates are also active in electoral politics. Today's interest groups understand that promoting their interests may hinge on electing new policymakers who support their position. With the help of professional staff or consultants interest groups may set up political action committees that contribute to individual candidates or help finance independent advocacy campaigns on behalf of their specific interests or those of their allies. This dimension of interest group activity is also discussed in Chapter 10.

Career Profile: Gerrie Benedi

Gerrie Benedi is a Government Affairs Representative with the National Association for Suppliers of Printing, Publishing and Converting Technologies, based in Reston, Virginia. Her association represents the interests of small business people in the printing field. As a professional in government affairs, Gerrie promotes her association's interests before U.S. Senators and Representatives and their staffs, and before members of executive branch agencies. Gerrie considers herself a lobbyist in the traditional sense, and more:

> My typical week, when Congress is in session,
> involves going to meetings downtown with our
> group's members, and with policymakers and their
> staffs. We are primarily concerned with looking
> out for the broad interests of our small business
> people, for example, how will a cut in the Estate
> Tax help them? I also spend a lot time back in my
> office writing 'action alerts' or press releases.
> Writing is a big part of my job, and you write to

many audiences. The challenge is to get their attention on important issues, which requires creativity. [2]

Unlike many governmental affairs offices, Gerrie's office usually works 9 a.m. to 5 p.m., although when an issue is up before Congress all staff are expected to stay until it's resolved. Gerrie cites many positive sides to her profession that make it likely she will continue to work as a lobbyist for many years:

> I like my job because you get to work on a lot of different issues and with many different people. I not only work directly with members of Congress and their staff, but with people at the local level who really appreciate my efforts on their behalf. I also attended some great political events, including three at the White House where President Bush spoke. I got to see him sign the bill on Trade Promotion Authority, and he was about three feet away from me.

Before starting her current position, Gerrie worked for several other groups including the National Beer Wholesalers Association. While working full time she earned her undergraduate degree in Government and Politics in 2000. Her advice to students interested in pursuing a similar position is to gain experience in government first, so you can see how policies are developed in the political process. According to Gerrie:

> To break into lobbying it's important to first experience how legislation gets passed. But you don't have to come to Washington to get that experience. Working in a legislator's district office, or in a state legislative or state executive office will help you prepare for a position in this field. Also, it's not just what you know, but who you know. During my internship and part-time jobs I met all kinds of people, and I continue to meet people who can be helpful to me later in my career.

Public and Media Relations

The fields of public and media relations overlap with traditional lobbying, although many public relations specialists and media directors are not considered lobbyists in the traditional sense. James Albertine, President of the American League of Lobbyists, affirms the central role of public relations within the larger interest advocacy profession: "Part of the job of a good lobbyist is PR. It's critical, in my view, that lobby campaigns put the best face on issues, goals and motives…It simply enhances your ability to get the word out."[3] Like traditional lobbyists, public relations and media specialists are found in government, in for-profit corporations and businesses, and in nonprofit organizations.[4]

Public relations positions in governments at the local, state and national level include *press secretary, information officer,* and *communications specialist.* These professionals disseminate information about government programs and activities to the public, and to other government agencies. For example, a governor's press secretary might work on short and long-term communication's projects including daily press briefings and drafting the governor's annual "state of the state" speech.

In addition to representing government entities, public relations specialists represent the interests of consumers, employees, and investors. They do this in a variety of ways including writing press releases, drafting speeches for their organization's leaders or key spokespersons, and promoting news stories or magazine articles. At the same time, PR specialists constantly work to keep their organization's management informed of public attitudes and possible changes in public policy at the local, state and national level.

According to the Public Relations Society of America, public relations encompass the following activities:[5]

- Anticipating, analyzing and interpreting public opinion, attitudes, and issues that might impact, for good or ill, the operations and plans of the organization.

- Counseling management at all levels in the organization with regard to policy decisions, courses of action, and communications, taking into account their public ramifications and the organization's social or citizenship responsibilities.

- Researching, conducting, and evaluating, on a continuing basis, programs of action and communication to achieve the informed public understanding necessary to success of an organization's aims. These may include marketing, financial, fund raising, employee, community or government relations, and other programs.

- Planning and implementing the organization's efforts to influence or change public policy. Setting objectives, planning, budgeting, recruiting and training staff, developing facilities-in short, managing the resources needed to perform all of the above.

Pursuing a Career in Interest Advocacy
There are several potential paths to becoming a professional in the field of interest advocacy. Experience working in legislatures or government agencies is almost a necessary prerequisite to getting hired as a lobbyist or public relations specialist in government. Internships or entry-level administrative positions in a legislative or governmental setting can provide a good start. If you are interested in media relations, you might first try working under a press secretary of a state legislator or member of Congress.

Many legislative or executive agency staffers utilize the so-called "revolving door" by working for a few years in government and then parlaying that experience into a position in interest group advocacy. In many cases these individuals specialize in the same issues they mastered while in government, and some even lobby their former government colleagues. For example, a senior staff member of a commerce committee in a state legislature may choose to work for a trade association that frequently has issues before that committee. While state or federal regulations may govern how soon someone can directly lobby those he or she used to work with, such restrictions are usually not that stringent. It takes strategy, persistence, and perhaps a little luck to become a lobbyist, government affairs specialist, press secretary, or other highly coveted positions within the field of interest advocacy. Aspiring interest advocates must hone their oral and written communications skills so they can boil down complex regulations or pieces of legislation into quick summary form. They must also have an intimate understanding of the nuances of legislative and executive regulatory processes. Finally, the most successful interest advocates have high-level "people skills" that either come naturally (some individuals are born "people persons") or are developed through years of work in the field.

While there is no one educational path to a career in interest advocacy, most professionals in this field have completed at least an undergraduate education, while an increasing number have attained graduate degrees. In addition to political science, other majors found in interest advocacy include law, communications, history, public administration or public relations.

Employment Trends
According to the U.S. Bureau of Labor Statistics,[6] there were 137,000 jobs held by interest advocates in 2000, with about six out of ten professionals working in service industries including management and public relations firms, membership organizations, educational institutions, and social service agencies. A smaller proportion worked for communications firms, financial institutions, and government agencies. Out of the total number of professionals employed in the field, about 8,600 were self-employed.

Employment in the broad field of interest advocacy is expected to increase much faster than the average for all occupations through 2010, according the U.S. Bureau of Labor Statistics. A significant proportion of new work on behalf of public and private organizations will be contracted out to firms rather than conducted through full-time support staff. Competition for entry-level jobs will remain fierce simply because there are more qualified applicants than job openings, and the avenues for entry into the field are numerous.

In 2000, the median annual salary for professionals in interest advocacy was $39,580, with the middle 50 percent of workers earning between

$29,610 and $53,620, and the upper 10 percent earning more than $70,480. Median annual earnings for private sector professionals are higher ($43,690) than median earnings for local government ($40,760) or state government ($39,560).

Additional Resources

- The American League of Lobbyists (ALL) is a membership organization dedicated to advancing the interests of the lobbying profession. The group's website, found at <www.alldc.org>, provides an overview of the interest advocacy profession and updated information on issues that affect lobbyists.

- Women in Government Relations, Inc. (WGR) is dedicated to promoting the professional and educational development of women in governmental relations. WGR offers annual professional development seminars, including its "Young Women's Seminar on Careers in Public Policy," and sponsors the WGR LEADER Foundation, an eight-month skills and leadership training program. WGR's website, at <www.wgr.org> offers information on these and other programs.

- With over 20, 000 members and 117 chapters, the Public Relations Society of America (PRSA) is the world's largest association of public relations professionals. Its website, at <www.prsa.org>, provides a detailed overview of the profession, employment opportunities, and professional development activities.

---

[1] Interview with the author.

[2] Interview with the author.

[3] Interview with *The Hill* newspaper, <www.alldc.org/0109face_to_face.htm>. Accessed 11-9-02.

[4] The following information was derived from the *Occupational Outlook Handbook*, U.S. Department of Labor. Additional information about careers in lobbying and public relations, including salary trends and employment statistics, can be found at <www.bls.gov>.

[5] <www.prsa.org/_Resources/Profession/>.

9. Print and Electronic Media

Print and electronic journalism encompass a variety of communications formats including print, radio, television and the Internet. There are numerous opportunities for political science majors in these fields. This chapter will identify some opportunities and provide guidance to students in how to supplement their political science education with further training and on-the-job experience.

Employment opportunities in print and electronic journalism for political science majors are substantial, although the competitive nature of media careers necessitates a creative and assertive approach to gaining employment. According to the U.S. Bureau of Labor Statistics[1], news analysts, reporters and correspondents held approximately 78,000 jobs in 2000. Half of these worked for newspapers, over one-quarter worked in radio and television broadcasting, and the remaining were self-employed or worked for news magazines and wire services.

Print Journalism
Newspapers and magazines have always played an essential role in America's representative democracy. The freedom of the press, as enshrined in the First Amendment to the U.S. Constitution, remains a cornerstone of free government. Despite the rise of electronic communications in the form of TV, cable, and the Internet, newspapers still represent the third largest industry in the U.S., employing about 450,000 people in various positions and departments including news, editorial, advertising, production, and circulation.[2] Currently, there are approximately 10,500 newspapers in the U.S., but only 39 have a circulation of more than 250,000. Thus, reporting and writing positions in large newspapers are scarce and very competitive, while such positions in smaller dailies and weeklies are more numerous.

Political science students who have a strong interest in daily news and who have strong writing and analytical thinking skills might consider a career in print journalism. There are several basic positions in newspaper publishing, including reporters and staff writers. *Reporters* cover a great variety of news events at the local, national, and international level, while *Staff writers* are reporters who are often assigned a specific "beat" focusing on things like politics, government, the arts, style, or consumer issues.

In addition to being strong writers, the best reporters are persistent, resourceful, detail-oriented, and have a "nose for news." Reporters often work irregular hours under pressing deadlines. Those who work for morning papers generally work from late afternoon until midnight. But many others must work nights, weekends and holidays. While reporters spend a lot of time at their desks writing under deadlines, reporting generally requires spending a lot of time outside the office researching stories, conducting interviews, and covering events. Some reporters accept hazardous assignments in politically unstable countries or in impoverished neighborhoods.

Obviously, a degree in journalism is the primary path to becoming a newspaper journalist. At the same time, newspapers need people from all backgrounds in the liberal arts. According to a study by the American Society of Newspaper Editors, about half of the editors surveyed had no preference for applicants with journalism degrees over those who majored in other fields.[3] Those surveyed also indicated that in addition to taking journalism courses such as basic reporting, copy-editing, and press law, coursework in economics and statistics is also valued. Editors look for candidates who have worked for their school newspapers, or who have gained on-the-job experience by interning at a newspaper. Many local newspapers will also consider publishing stories written by freelancers, also known as "stringers," who submit articles independently. Having a byline story in one or more local newspapers can strengthen your qualifications for newspaper work.

Most reporters and staff writers start at small newspapers and move up to more important assignments at larger newspapers as they accrue experience and prove themselves to their present and future employers. Competition is most keen for positions at large metropolitan newspapers and national magazines, while small town and suburban newspapers and weeklies offer the most opportunities for print journalists.

Because most newspapers rely on advertising revenue to survive, the newspaper industry is sensitive to national economic conditions. In recessionary times there are less positions open, and some journalists may be laid off.

Radio and Television

Despite increased competition from cable television and the Internet, radio continues to play a vital role in electronic broadcasting. While *disc jockeys* still announce for stations in all music formats, over the last three decades "talk radio" formats have proliferated across the country. Talk radio features prominent national or local personalities who weigh in on a number of topics, or host shows devoted to a particular subject such as politics, sports, mental and physical health, and even cars. Most of these shows employ low-paid researchers and assistant producers, and usually offer internships to college students seeking to gain radio production experience.

The basic "high profile" positions in television news include news analyst, reporter, and correspondent. *News analysts* compile news from various sources including wire services and local reporters. Also called *newscasters* or *news anchors*, news analysts prepare news stories for airing on broadcasts. *Reporters* investigate news leads, observe events, and interview people for news stories. Reporters may also write stories and report directly from the field for taped news packages or live broadcast. *Correspondents* generally report for larger news organizations and are often stationed in large U.S. or world cities.

Today most college students who are interested in television news aspire to be on-air anchors, reporters or correspondents at large network news stations. These are admirable goals. But the reality is that few ever make it that far. Most on-air opportunities are found at stations with smaller markets that often pay low salaries. Students interested in television should also consider "lower profile" positions in producing, technical operations, graphics, desk operations, and human resource management.

There are several outlets available to pursue a career in television news. The most obvious are local or national commercial or cable television stations. National television networks maintain bureaus in other countries that also employ individuals in these positions. Production companies that produce stories independently for television offer additional opportunities.

Many students who aspire to careers in broadcast journalism major in communications or journalism. But scores of professionals in the field today majored in other fields, including political science. News managers seek people who have broad knowledge, skills and experiences. Political science majors should strive to supplement their major courses with classes in advanced writing and journalism. They should also complete one or more internship as such entry-level work experience is widely considered necessary to gaining a paid position.

Career Profile: Lisa Havlovitz

Lisa Havlovitz is an Associate Producer at NBC Network News in Washington, DC. Her duties include researching guests and compiling footage for the Tim Russert Show, and assisting Tim Russert in his role as Washington Bureau Chief and moderator of Meet the Press. Lisa earned a bachelor's degree in political science from the University of California, Santa Barbara in 1993. As a student Lisa pursued her interest in broadcast news by taking extra writing and journalism classes, and interning at a local television station in Santa Barbara, California. Lisa learned a lot as an intern in local television, and has specific advice for others interested in broadcast journalism:

> While interning may not seem worth it at first, the payoff is usually greater than expected. Interning allows you to observe all facets of the TV news operation and helps you decide what path you want to pursue. If your interest is reporting you should try to find someone at the station who can mentor you. A seasoned reporter can be a great asset to an aspiring journalist. You might also try learning the technical aspects of television. The jobs may not be as glamorous as working in the newsroom, but they are the backbone of the news operation. Also, by learning one or more positions including director, floor director, camera operator or graphics you become more marketable as a job prospect. These skills keep you at the station where you can continue to pursue other passions such as reporting or anchoring.[4]

In the mid 1990s Lisa moved to Washington, DC to pursue jobs in television news. Her path to Associate Producer at NBC Network News offers a good example of how meandering the climb to a rewarding career can be. As Lisa explains:

I didn't have a job when I moved to Washington. So when I got here I cold-called all the radio and TV stations I could find to see if they had openings. None did at the time. A few weeks later a local radio station called me back looking for a part-time traffic director. [Radio traffic directors schedule all the commercials that are aired.] Of course, this wasn't my desired career, but I took it anyway to survive. Luckily for me the radio station was located in the NBC News building. It was just a matter of days before I was inquiring upstairs about entry-level jobs. After a month or so I was hired by NBC part time to answer the phones. This certainly wasn't a glamorous job, but it did help me learn about all the positions and people in the bureau. During these early months I worked extra hard, and always asked other people if they needed help. Tim Russert's assistant would often ask me do things for her, and I guess I was good at what I did because I got hired on full time at the phones. After a couple of years I was promoted to news operations coordinator. This is the person who schedules all the camera crews and other technical people. That job was really challenging, but very rewarding as well in that I got to learn about all facets of network news, including cameras, lighting, audio, satellite operations, and labor union regulations. The knowledge I gained in that position is still very useful to me now. After a couple of years on the technical side I was hired as an Associate Producer for the weekly Tim Russert show, and as Tim's personal assistant. My current position allows me to do a variety of things including researching guests and show topics and finding footage to air during the show. And as Tim Russert's assistant, I get to witness first-hand how network news covers big stories such as the 2000 presidential election stalemate, and the September 11 attacks.

In 2000 Lisa earned a Master's degree in broadcast journalism from American University, and NBC paid for half of her tuition. According to Lisa,

> one benefit of working for a large network is the tuition assistance they make available to employees. Without that assistance I would still be paying off my graduate school tuition. I benefit every day from what I learned at American, and NBC benefits from my advanced training too.

Lisa's story provides one example of how a political science graduate who works hard and maintains some flexibility in pursuing her goals can do quite well in a competitive field like broadcast journalism.

Alternative Media

Despite the significant growth of alternative media formats, such as web-based magazines including Salon and Slate, and websites devoted to news, politics and commentary, most Americans still get their news and other information from newspapers, television, and print magazines. Increasingly, however, people are accessing Internet sources and incorporating those sources into their regular routines. The appeal of Internet news is that it's fast and current. Thus, there is a growing market for writers, graphics specialists, and web designers in the field to keep these formats fresh and informative. Major promoters of news and public affairs websites include CNN, MSNBC, *Time*, and *Newsweek*, and several daily newspapers such as the *New York Times*, *The Washington Post*, and *The Los Angeles Times*. Political science graduates should already have a broad background in politics, public affairs, governmental institutions, and public policy. Those who are interested in new media formats should supplement their major courses with classes in HTML, Java, Adobe Photoshop, and other computer programs. Of course, these skills are not just applicable for jobs involving alternative media. Increasingly, employers in most career sectors value new hires who have such experience.

Salaries and Employment Trends

According to career expert Blythe Camenson, the combined yearly average salary of all print and electronic news analysts including newscasters, reporters, and correspondents is approximately $26,470, with the middle 50 percent earning between $19,210 and $40, 930. The lowest 10 percent earned less than $14,100 yearly, while the highest 10 percent earned over $70,140.[5] But according to the Bureau of Labor Statistics, radio and television salaries, when calculated on a per-hour basis, were lower than the average for all reporters and correspondents. For example, the average salary of on-air announcers in radio and television was relatively low, with median hourly earnings for radio and television announcers in 2000 being $9.54. The lowest 10 percent of announcers earned less than $5.94 hourly, while the highest earned over an average of $24.35, per hour.

The Bureau of Labor Statistics also predicts that increased consolidation of radio and television stations, coupled with the growth of alternative media sources such as web-based news magazines will contribute to a decline in the market for on-air announcers. In addition, increases in digital technology will decrease the need for off-air technical and production work. Overall, the Department of Labor projects that positions within the broadcast industry will increase by no more than ten percent between 1998 and 2010, which is much lower than the average for most other occupations it tracks. These trends suggest there will be an increased number of talented and qualified people chasing after fewer jobs. Students still interested in pursuing a career in radio or television broadcasting are well advised to accrue a range of experiences with various positions, including production, editing, and technical support to ensure their greatest marketability.

Additional Resources

- Jobs Page, found at <www.freep/jobspage/interns/>, is a one-stop resource for finding newspaper internships. Sponsored by the Detroit Free Press.

- General information on the broadcasting industry is provided by the National Association of Broadcasters, found at <www.nab.org>.

- The National Cable and Telecommunications Association website, at <www.ncta.com> offers statistics and career information about the cable industry.

- The Radio and Television News Directors Foundation website, at <www.rtndf.org> includes information about scholarships, careers, and job placement.

- *Women in Television News Revisited*, Marlane, Judith. Austin: University of Texas Press (1999).

---

[1] Unless otherwise indicated, position descriptions and statistics in this chapter are derived from the *Occupational Outlook Handbook*, U.S. Bureau of Labor Statistics. Found at <www.bls.gov>.

[2] Employment statistics for newspaper positions are derived from Blythe Camenson, *Great Jobs for Liberal Arts Majors*. New York: VGM Career Books (2002): 56.

[3] Survey results compiled in 1990, as reported at <www.asne.org/kiosk/careers/jartxt.htm>.

[4] Interview with the author.

[5] *Great Jobs for Liberal Arts Majors*, p. 161-162.

10. Campaigns and Polling

There are over 500,000 elective positions in the United States that form the backbone of America's representative democracy. Regular elections are held for mayors, city council members, county treasurers, school board members, sheriffs, governors, state legislators, U.S. representatives and senators, and president of the United States. In addition, scores of initiatives, referenda, and bond elections are held during each election cycle as well. Since virtually all elections are contested at the state, county or local level, there are ample opportunities to work in electoral politics no matter where you live.

The Benefits of Campaign Experience
If you talk with someone who regularly volunteers in electoral politics they are likely to tell you how rewarding campaign work can be. While the pay ranges from little to nothing, the payoffs are great. Elections offer direct opportunities to engage in representative or direct democracy. The vast majority of campaign workers volunteer part-time because they believe in their candidate or issue and want to participate directly in the democratic process. Even though elections inevitably produce winners and losers, the process itself can be very satisfying even if your candidate or issue falls short on election night.

In addition to its ample civic rewards, campaign work offers several paths for career development. First, many people consider campaign work a necessary prerequisite to gaining a full-time paid job in politics or government. Campaigns typically offer more responsibility, sooner, than jobs in the private sector. Many state legislators and members of Congress, for example, look first to their campaign staff when hiring for their district or legislative offices. And why shouldn't they? Unpaid campaign workers have already demonstrated loyalty and a commitment to their candidate's stand on important issues. They have also proved themselves to be good workers who have the requisite skills and experiences to serve their bosses well.

Second, campaign workers often form a camaraderie and common sense of purpose that lasts well beyond election day. Thus, working in electoral politics is an excellent way to make contacts with people who share similar interests. Such contacts can be invaluable for finding political jobs and positioning yourself to best compete for those jobs. For example, many White House employees gained their first political experience as campaign volunteers, as the career profile below will illustrate.

Finally, people with extensive campaign experience are most qualified for professional campaign positions including campaign manager, pollster, and campaign consultant. They are also good prospects for non-electoral positions in political interest groups such as the National Rifle Association, the American Association of Retired Persons, labor unions, as well as public relations and consulting firms.

The Nature of Campaign Work

You don't have to wait until your junior or senior year to work in elections. On the contrary, some of the best campaign workers started out in high school or earlier as volunteers. Because they have an initial interest in government and politics, and are developing a basic knowledge about political and electoral processes, political science majors are particularly suited for campaign work. Generally, the more campaign experience you accrue, the more responsibilities and opportunities you are given. But even workers with several campaigns under their belt will pitch in on phone banks or neighborhood canvassing when needed.

The smaller campaign organizations are usually run by a *campaign manager* who is responsible for organizing the campaign and, depending on the size of the campaign, will work on fundraising, events planning, and press relations. Basic tasks in the campaign will likely include fundraising, phone banking, conducting mass mailings, and canvassing from door-to-door. In small local campaigns the candidate and often his or her family will work side-by-side with volunteers to get these jobs done. Because everyone pitches in on various tasks in smaller campaigns, the opportunities to gain experience in many campaign functions may be greater than working in large campaign organizations.

Larger campaign organizations will often hire individuals for a few professional positions that are coordinated by the campaign manager or outside political consultant. These positions might include *press secretary, pollster, fundraiser, treasurer,* and *coordinator of direct mailings*. A candidate for higher office such as U.S. representative, senator, or governor, might hire a political consulting firm to handle all or most of these basic functions.

Career Profile: Brianna Wilkins and Donald Leonard
While undergraduates at Michigan State University, Brianna Wilkins and Donald Leonard each worked in their first political campaigns during the 2002 mid-term elections. Brianna worked for Tim Bishop's successful campaign for Congress in New York, while Donald worked for Erskine Bowle's unsuccessful campaign for U.S. Senate in North Carolina. Both students found their campaign experiences rewarding and worthwhile.

Brianna was recruited for campaign work through the 21st Century Democrats, an affiliate group of the Democratic Party. "I had a choice between campaigns in Minnesota, South Dakota, New Jersey or New York. I chose the New York option because it sounded like they really needed me there," explains Brianna. Because Brianna joined the campaign effort in the last week before the election, she had to hit the ground running:

> I started by canvassing with a team of students
> from all over for ten hours a day. Basically our
> message was 'Ritchie is bad, vote for Tim.'
> Although last-minute canvassing was hard, I saw
> that it really mattered. It was a great feeling to see
> people you talked to actually getting to the polls.
> We had an 86 percent turnout, which is incredible
> when you compare that to the national average.
> Would I volunteer again? In a heartbeat. I'm
> definitely planning to join up with another
> campaign in two years, although next time I will
> get started earlier.[1]

Like Brianna, Donald was placed on a campaign in its last week. Originally, Donald planned to work in Pennsylvania, but at the last minute he was offered a stipend to work on the Bowles' campaign in North Carolina, so he took it:

> When I got there I was assigned a particular
> county to organize, along with two other students.
> Basically, we were told to build a 'get out the vote
> effort' from the ground up. They gave us phone
> cards, and money to recruit workers at $50 a day.
> We began by contacting area organizations such

as the local NAACP, and churches. We said, 'you know the area, we don't. So please help us,' and many did. In the last days of the campaign we had over 50 people working for us each day. We all basically targeted different neighborhoods to urge people to get out and vote.[2]

Even though his candidate lost the election, Donald still considers his week of campaign work "one of the best experiences I've had." And like Brianna, Donald plans to work on another campaign in 2004.

Related Campaign and Electoral Opportunities
As discussed in Chapter 8, many interest groups are involved in electoral politics directly, or engage in electoral activities through support of political action committees or political party organizations. Political groups including trade associations, labor unions, public interest and single-issue groups hire individuals with substantial campaign experience to engage in electioneering that may or may not be coordinated with the parties or candidate organization. EMILY's List, for example, is a liberal pro-choice group that supports pro-choice women candidates by identifying viable candidates, raising money, and providing technical campaign support. More conservative organizations that often align their efforts with the Republican Party or individual conservative candidates include the Eagle Forum and the Christian Coalition.

Political action committees (PACs) are major players in electoral politics that offer paid opportunities for people with substantial campaign experience. Created and sponsored by interest groups, labor unions, trade associations, and even individual office holders, PACs gather monetary contributions together and redistribute them to candidates in a coordinated way. Whether you consider PACs unworthy tools of "special interests" or legitimate vehicles for more effective democratic participation, the reality is that PACs are and will remain key players in electoral politics.

Political parties and their affiliated organizations at the national and state level engage in various electioneering activities including candidate recruitment, training, fundraising, advertising, mobilizing campaign supporters and get-out-the-vote drives. Parties spend a lot of money and effort to get their candidates elected, or their office holders reelected. While paid positions are scarce in the periods between elections, interns and volunteers who are willing to invest the time and make a strong effort can often find a paid position. Once again, experience in campaigns or involvement in campus party organizations will make you a better job prospect. Be aware, however, that party workers are generally expected be consistent in their partisan activities. For example, a lifelong Democratic activist is not likely to get hired by a Republican candidate or campaign committee, and vice versa.

There are also ample opportunities for volunteer or paid work for individuals who consider themselves independents, or who belong to a third party. "Independents" and third party supporters can find meaningful work in support of a particular ballot initiative or referendum, in working for a particular candidate, or working on behalf of a third party. Several third parties, including the Green Party, the Libertarian Party, and the Reform Party, nominate candidates at the local and sometimes state level, advocate for local ballot initiatives, and engage in extensive grassroots organization efforts between and during election periods. What keeps supporters working for third parties is a strong commitment to issues and a belief that their party can make a difference. Third party advocates are quick to remind critics that the Republicans were once a third party as well.

Political consulting, polling and communications firms also offer substantial professional opportunities for experienced job candidates. Consulting firms specialize in one or a few functions such as advertising, focus groups and polling, while others provide a wide range of services to include strategic planning, advertising, media buys, fundraising and government lobbying. Some firms are more partisan than others.

Consulting firms that are identified with the Republican Party include:
Wirthlin Worldwide
McAulliffe Message Media
Sandler-Innocenzi

Consulting firms that are identified with the Democratic Party include:
Trippi McMahon & Squier
Dixon-Davis Media
Murphy Putnam
Shrum Donilon Devine
Doak, Carrier and O'Donnell

Polling firms gauge public opinion using polls, focus groups, and other opinion tracking methods.

Those that are identified with the Republican Party include:

Public Opinion Strategies
American Viewpoint
Linda Divall
John McLaughlin
Market Strategies

Polling firms that are identified with the Democratic Party include:

Mellman Group
Penn Schoen & Berland
Bennett Petts & Blumenthal
Peter Hart
Celinda Lake

Media groups such as ABC, CNBC, CNN/Time, *Wall Street Journal*, and *Los Angeles Times* regularly conduct polls as well.

Career Profile: Susan Oglinsky

Susan Oglinsky is currently with Greener and Hook, a Washington-based political consulting firm. She is a good example of someone whose volunteer work in political campaigns provided the necessary experiences and contacts to attain fulfilling paid positions in campaigns, government and political consulting. Susan is just one of many political science students who has built a rewarding career in the dynamic world of electoral politics.

In the middle 1990s, Susan began working as a volunteer for several Republican candidates in her home state of Virginia. She then interned in the Virginia office of Representative Tom Davis (R-VA) in 1995, where she did research, provided office support, and assisted staff in community outreach. In 1996, Susan joined Rep. Davis's reelection campaign where she honed her campaign skills including community outreach and debate preparation. For the next four years Susan worked as a campaign staff member on several Republican campaigns, and in the office of a Virginia State Delegate where she gained experience researching and tracking legislation, doing constituent service, and acting as a liaison between the delegate and the many lobbyists who contacted her office. Susan believes these early volunteer and entry-level positions were instrumental in preparing her for political positions with more responsibility:

> I gained a lot from my early campaign and state legislative work. In campaign work the rewards are great, even when your candidate loses. You can make such an impact in the short few months of the campaign. Something you do benefits the campaign every day, and you can see the results of your efforts. You also see where you make mistakes, and are able to correct them the next time around. In electoral politics it's very important to get this kind of experience on your resume, and this type of experience usually trumps other things such as formal schooling. Also, the contacts I made during these early years were invaluable to me later on. [3]

Susan also learned that it takes passion and commitment to succeed in electoral politics:

> When deciding where to volunteer, don't just look for the person whom you think will win. You should have something in common with your candidate. It helps a lot when you are defending his or her beliefs. Try to work with someone who has character and a good reputation. In politics, you have to be careful about whom you are aligned with.

By the early 2000s, Susan was taking on more responsibilities as a campaign manager for a Republican candidate, and as a PAC assistant for the International Paper Political Action Committee. In these positions Susan learned a lot about the fundraising side of electoral politics. When an early campaign co-worker became an associate political director in the Bush White House, he urged her to apply for a position in the White House Office of Political Affairs. She did, and was hired as an assistant to her former campaign contact. While at the White House Susan helped plan campaign events and opposition research for various Republican candidates, and assisted the associate director in writing political briefs. In 2002, Susan started her current position at Greener and Hook.

Susan Oglinsky is just one among countless political science students who worked their way up through the world of electoral politics. Perhaps most impressive about Susan's story is the fact that she did all of these things while still completing her undergraduate degree!

Additional Resources
- The American Association of Political Consultants, found at <www.theaapc.org> is a bipartisan association comprised of professionals in a variety of campaign specialties.

- Politics1.Com bills itself as "the most comprehensive online guide to American politics." Its website, at <www.politics1.com> contains extensive resources and links organized by parties, issues and political ideologies. Included are links to conservative and liberal political consultants, and numerous opportunities to work in electoral politics.

- Project Vote Smart , at <www.vote-smart.org>, bills itself as "the last trusted source for political information." It maintains a national library of information on over 13,000 elected offices and candidates for public office.

- Rock the Vote sponsors a host of initiatives including issues forums, citizen action training, and get-out-the- vote initiatives. Found at <www.rockthevote.org>.

- Democratic Congressional Campaign Committee, <www.dccc.org>.

- National Republican Campaign Committee, <www.nrcc.org>.

- Democratic Senatorial Campaign Committee, <www.dscc.org>.

- National Republican Senatorial Committee, <www.nrsc.org>.

---

[1] Interview with the author, and class comments.
[2] Interview with the author, and class comments.
[3] Interview with the author.

11. For-Profit Organizations

A common misnomer is that people with political science degrees are poor candidates for business careers. In fact, nothing could be further from the truth. A quick web search reveals a host of recent promotions for former political science majors in the world of business. For example, political science graduates were recently hired or promoted into the following positions and companies: Vice President and General Manager, Warner Home Video (*Business Wire*, 1-13-03); Executive Vice President, Vivendi (*Business Wire*, 1-8-03); Board of Directors, Gladstone Capital (*Global News Wire*, 1-6-03); President and Vice Chair, White & Baldacci (*The Washington Post*, 1-6-03); Board of Directors, Informatica (*PR Newswire*, 1-3-03); Vice President and General Manager, Dell Networking (*Network World*, 12-30-02). A majority of political science graduates today are employed in the for-profit sector, with about one-third of graduates working in traditional business careers.[1] Because the for-profit career options open to political science graduates are so broad and varied, this chapter can only highlight a few major sectors. Students interested in a business career should do additional research, starting with the resources listed at the end of this chapter.

The Nature of For-Profit Organizations
In contrast to nonprofits, for-profit organizations are driven by the bottom line of profits generated by selling products and services that others want. Unlike governments, for-profit businesses maintain direct control over their own budgets, personnel, and modes of production. While some for-profits are publicly owned, and therefore must answer to shareholders, the managers of publicly owned companies still enjoy greater discretion than managers in governments or nonprofit organizations.

Besides traditional business opportunities, careers in the for-profit sector include positions in advertising, marketing, and management consulting. These opportunities are briefly introduced below. Students interested in one or more of these fields should explore these opportunities further. A list of resources at the end of the chapter can provide a good start.

Business careers are found in a range of venues, from small family-owned entities that can be very innovative and entrepreneurial to large multinational corporations that can be very bureaucratic. The majority of businesses in the U.S. have less than 500 employees. Whether they are just starting out or are long established, businesses and their products are subject to many governmental regulations at the local, national and even international level. Thus, there is a need for employees who understand public sector politics and regulatory processes. For example, large automobile or paper manufacturers must comply with scores of federal environmental regulations that are passed by Congress and enforced by the Environmental Protection Agency, and numerous state and local regulations as well. Corporate offices that deal with regulatory affairs employ researchers, lawyers, and government liaisons to track regulations and work towards their most favorable interpretation. As discussed in Chapter 5, graduates with a specialty in international relations might be good candidates to work for multinational corporations, or smaller domestic businesses that are looking to expand their markets overseas. In addition, graduates with a specialty in public administration may be good candidates for personnel management or human resources divisions in small, medium and large sized businesses.

Executives are at the top of the business hierarchy, and thus are among the highest paid business professionals. Specific job titles for business executives include *chief executive officer*, *president*, *board chair*, or *chief operating officer*. While salaries range from very good to excellent for business executives, the responsibilities and pressures of these positions are equally great. Top executives are responsible for earning higher profits for the organization or shareholders, and often shoulder the blame when profits fall short of projections. Frequent travel and job transfers are also expected of executives in large corporations.

In order to identify and attract talented college graduates, many corporations maintain active college recruiting programs that utilize campus job fairs and interview programs. Corporate recruiters will often review resumes from students in a broad range of majors. Your political science program provides some basic tools for working in the for-profit world including strong writing, effective public speaking, a capacity for critical thinking, and a broad knowledge of public-sector institutions and public policy. To better position yourself for this career sector, you should seriously consider adding a minor in business or a related field including economics or finance. Introductory and advanced courses in economics, mathematics, budgeting, finance, marketing, advertising, public relations and information technology are useful additions to your basic general education and political science requirements. Increasingly, businesses are adding "e-commerce" capabilities to their operations, which may include operations to advertise, take orders, and receive payments electronically. Job candidates with hard skills involving e-commerce, such as website design and programming may gain an edge over other applicants. Students interested in business careers should also immerse themselves in business practices, issues and trends. One way to start doing this is to regularly read business newspapers and periodicals including *The Wall St. Journal*, *Business Week*, and *Fortune*. Political science majors should also pursue internship or corporate training opportunities in business.

Career Trends in Business

Because the business world is so diverse, different sectors are subject to various factors that can affect their potential growth. Thus, it is impossible to project employment trends for the entire business world. However, it is useful to remember that national or global economic booms and recessions can affect most business activity. In strong economies, for example, consumers have more money to spend on goods and services, which can impact businesses in one or more stages in their chain of supply and demand. During this environment businesses may choose to expand to meet these new demands for their products or services. Slower economic activity, on the other hand, means that consumers are spending less, which may necessitate layoffs in the business sector. Often the first employees to go are those involved in advertising, research and new product development, and those with the least seniority. One trend that will likely continue is the rapid increase of new technology needs for most businesses. Thus, employees with more advanced technology skills will remain integral to successful business survival and growth.

Consulting

Business consultants work in a wide range of for-profit and public-sector settings including materials management, finance and accounting, administrative services, marketing, logistics, information technology, government contracting and procurement. Consultants analyze management problems and propose solutions that are in keeping with the organization's goals and values. Individual projects vary widely depending on the client and the consultant's specialty.

To be effective, consultants must be self-starters who can work under little or no supervision. Strong analytical and people skills are also considered a must, as are team building and oral and written communications skills.

Consultants can expect to work long hours when deadlines loom, and some must travel frequently. Many consultants are employed through large consulting firms including Deloitte Consulting, Booz Allen & Hamilton, and Ernst & Young. The employment prospects for consultants are relatively good as job growth is expected to be above average through 2006.[2]

Career Profile: Ernie Chung

Ernie Chung is a consultant at Booz Allen & Hamilton, one of the largest and oldest consulting firms in the world. His office, which does both public and private sector management and organizational consulting, is based in Mclean, Virginia. The U.S. Navy is his firm's oldest client. Ernie, who earned his bachelor's degree in political science and international relations in 1997, describes his experiences with public sector consulting this way:

> I like public sector consulting because it's always different. You work independently or on small teams, depending on the project. After working a problem I make recommendations to the client to do certain things to fix it. Sometimes they act on your recommendations, sometimes they don't. Public sector consulting is not always driven by the bottom line, and there is less pressure to work 80-hour weeks. You can do interesting things like they do on the commercial side, but work half the hours.[3]

Ernie's indirect path to Booz Allen & Hamilton reaffirms the opportunities for political science graduates in both public sector and commercial consulting.

> After graduation I worked for a couple of years in the Washington office of Senator Diane Feinstein. While I was there I realized I was more interested in business than politics. Even though I didn't have a business or accounting background I applied to Booz Allen & Hamilton through monster.com. Although I didn't get the original job I applied for, they kept my resume and called

104

me in to interview for my current position. In hindsight, I would have been a stronger applicant if I had some evidence of analytical or finance skills. But they did like my communications skills.

Ernie plans to apply to an MBA program in the future. Although his formal background isn't business, his experience with Booz Allen & Hamilton will surely be an asset: "My current position should be a nice springboard to an MBA since business schools want people with real-world experience," explains Ernie.

Advertising, Marketing and Public Relations

Despite their many differences, the fields of advertising, marketing and public relations each involve shaping peoples' perceptions of products and services.[4] Whether the product is a soft drink, a management-training program, or a public service message, concept development and promotion remain essential elements of a firm's success. Thus, there will always be a need for creative and hard working professionals in these fields.

Advertising involves creating or articulating the essential concepts behind products and developing the words and images that make up product advertisements. Advertising jobs include *copywriters*, *art directors*, and *account executives*. Political science graduates may be particularly suited to public interest campaigns, for example, those promoting seat belt use or anti-drug messages. Such campaigns are often sponsored by national, state or local governments, or created and managed by firms contracted to provide such services. To qualify for an advertising career a political science student should supplement his or her major program of study with a minor in advertising or graphic arts, or with substantial on-the-job experiences in the advertising field.

Marketing involves brand and product management, sales, and product research, design, and distribution. Some marketing professionals are generalists, while others specialize in one or more of the essential elements of marketing. Traditionally associated with consumer products, marketing is increasingly important for nonprofit organizations such as museums and colleges, government agencies, and even nations. Most professionals in middle or upper-level marketing positions have acquired a master's degree in business administration (MBA) or worked their way up from entry-level marketing research positions. Political science students interested in domestic or international marketing careers should consider adding a minor in business or marketing.

Public relations professionals are the link between organizations and the general public. As discussed in Chapter 8, public relations has become an essential function in nearly all public and private-sector organizations including corporations of all sizes, governments, labor unions, trade associations, environmental organizations, and educational institutions. According to career expert Blythe Camenson:

> The information industry outranks any other and in the last four decades and has become the central nucleus of the United States economy and its labor force. More workers are now employed in some facet of the information industry than in any other sector…Some sectors need to get the message out in-house, through newsletters, memos, position papers, letters from the president, corporate training, seminars, and workshops; other sectors need to get the message out to the public or to consumers, through conventions, advertisements, publicity campaigns, community relations, or media contacts.[5]

To prepare for a career in public relations, political science majors should consider adding a minor or taking electives in communications, journalism, or media studies.

Additional Resources

- *Management Consulting: A Complete Guide to the Industry.* S. Biswas and D. Twitchell (1999).

- *Encyclopedia of Business and Finance.* B. Kaliski, ed. (2001).

- The Careers in Business website, found at <www.careers-in-business.com>, includes resources for students to explore a variety of business careers.

- For information about marketing careers, visit <www.careers-in-marketing.com>.

- The American Marketing Association, found at <www.ama.org>, provides information about careers, industry trends, and training in marketing.

- The International Advertising Association, which describes itself as "a global and grass roots community of successful brand builders, offers news, resources and links at its website, found at <www.iaaglobal.org>.

---

[1] Employment statistic reported at <www.bradley.edu/pls.html>.
[2] Department of Labor trends as reported at <careers.cua.edu>.
[3] Interview with the author.
[4] Job sector descriptions derived from information provided at <www.collegegrad.com>, <www.careers.cua.edu>, and <www.bls.gov>.
[5] *Great Jobs for Liberal Arts Majors.* New York: VGM Career Books, (2002), p. 133.

12. Public Service and Elective Office

Some Americans bemoan that we live in an "age of cynicism" where citizens don't care for their neighbors and choose not to contribute anything to their communities or country. While it's a fact that many people are apathetic and uninvolved, the spirit of public service remains strong in the U.S. Just look around; there are numerous examples of public service activities in your local community.

The term "public service" spans a wide range of volunteer, appointive and elective positions and activities. The discussion of government careers in Chapters 3 and 4, and nonprofit careers in Chapter 6 make clear that individuals can make a decent living by working in public service. This chapter explores other dimensions of public service not covered elsewhere in this book including the numerous volunteer, appointive and elective positions open to college students, recent graduates, and even those with full-time jobs.

Volunteer Activities
People with a passion for public service don't have to neglect their civic values while they attend school or work in another career field. Most public service activities are voluntary and pursued by people with full-time careers. Millions of citizens volunteer part-time as tutors, coaches, fundraisers, administrators, and in countless other ways in the U.S. and around the world. Besides deriving satisfaction from giving back something to their communities or nation, volunteers also gain significant skills, work experiences and contacts that can directly benefit them personally.

Obviously, the immense range of volunteer opportunities cannot be adequately covered in a few pages. This section discusses three opportunities that may be of particular interest to political science majors: local neighborhood associations, parent/teacher associations (PTAs), and political parties. Additional resources for students interested in other forms of public service are provided at the end of the chapter.

Political science graduates with an interest in local government or public policy may be particularly suited to volunteer for their local civic or neighborhood associations. Despite the potential impact of local issues on their daily lives, most citizens consider themselves too busy to play a role in community planning or neighborhood advocacy. Increasingly, local communities must grapple with growing populations, strained roads and infrastructure, and rampant development. Thus, there will always be a need for committed and knowledgeable participants. Neighborhood associations offer significant opportunities for local involvement in community planning issues.

Local citizen advisory boards and study groups offer additional ways to engage in public service and participate in local governance. Cities, townships and counties often commission study groups to examine issues such as pedestrian safety, business development, or affordable housing. Members investigate the issues and make recommendations for change to local government officials. Because of limited public resources, local policymakers rely heavily on citizens who volunteer their time and skills to make sure that public needs are met.

Local PTAs provide additional avenues for citizen involvement in educational issues, especially for those with school-aged children. Since education is a major and ongoing commitment of government, PTAs at the local or regional level will continue to play a central role in developing education policy. Communities across the nation are currently dealing with significant education issues including standardized testing, teacher certification standards, charter schools, and budget shortfalls in an era of shrinking local resources. An individual's involvement in PTAs, or in a local school or school district can make a big difference.

State and local political party organizations also provide substantial opportunities for volunteers who yearn to participate in politics. Because local party meetings are often sparsely attended, and many local positions remain vacant, there are substantial opportunities to get involved in local politics. Many current high-level party leaders and elected officials started out as volunteers in local party committees. Their early work in politics allowed them to pursue their interest in electoral politics while also making the contacts that were necessary for gaining higher positions with more responsibility and influence. In addition to local and state party organizations, national party organizations, including 21st Century Democrats and College Republicans offer additional volunteer, internship, and paid opportunities.

Third parties also offer great opportunities for political science students who yearn to get involved. Studies suggest that young people today are less likely to identify strongly with the Democrats or Republicans than past generations. However, new technologies including the Internet and mass mailings have contributed to a proliferation of parties and independent political advocacy organizations. Third parties such as the Libertarian Party, the Green Party, and the Reform Party develop issue platforms, recruit and run candidates, and engage in various electioneering activities including fundraising, voter registration and turnout programs, and petition drives in support of candidates, referenda and initiatives. Independent political advocacy and "good government" organizations, including Common Cause, Project Vote Smart, and the League of Women Voters also offer avenues for political participation. Committed volunteers are essential for the successful operation of all parties and independent political groups.

Career Profile: John Seymour

John Seymour is a good example of an active citizen who pursues public service in both his full-time paid work and his numerous volunteer activities. John currently works for the Southern California Housing Development Corporation, a nonprofit corporation that builds or renovates affordable housing units in the vast Southern California region. As John sees it, his job provides an essential public service given the high costs of California rental properties:

> Our projects typically take two years from start to finish. We work with cities that are open to developing affordable housing by first deciding whether renovation of existing units is the best option, or whether new construction makes more sense. We then go hunting for space and project funding, and work with the city councils to set up the legal agreements. My job is very challenging, but also extremely rewarding in that local residents who can't afford to buy at market prices now have other housing options.[1]

John supplements his nonprofit career with extensive volunteer work in political campaigns and local community affairs. In addition to working on several Republican campaigns over the years, John served for three years as chair of his local community planning board, and as a board member for another two years. According to John, the planning board played an important role in charting the direction of his San Diego community for decades to come:

> There are 26 local boards in San Diego. We review all local issues including new housing developments, and monitor building code violations. Basically we act as watchdogs in our particular area. Our biggest issue was the closing of the 500-acre Naval Training Center, which was located in our community and sat adjacent to Lindberg field, our city's main airport. The question before us was: What should be done with the land? Everyone weighed in with different plans. The airport people wanted to expand the airport. The local Indian tribe wanted to create Indian housing and a gaming facility. Other locals wanted more park space. We worked with all these stakeholders to develop a master plan calling for mixed land use including more Navy housing, a community recreation center, an arts walk, and retail and park space. This area is now called Liberty Station, and most everyone seems happy with the outcome.

John's interest in public service and local affairs motivated him to run for San Diego City Council in 1995:

> I was motivated to run because through my community work on land use issues, I saw there was a need for a more balanced approach to land use in the larger San Diego area. I thought about running for two years, and campaigned actively for one year prior to the general election. I raised $210,000 in small direct contributions from over 2000 people, and had a full-time campaign manager and assistant manager, and over 20 committed volunteers. The best part of this experience wasn't all the media attention on

election night; it was the unconditional backing of my wife who early on said she was proud of me no matter whether I won or lost. Another great thing was walking door-to-door. Although it was hard doing this every day between 3pm and dark, and all day on the weekends, it was a great feeling to meet people who supported your issues and said they would vote for you.

Unfortunately, John came in a close second on election night. Local political experts, however, considered this a strong showing given that it was John's first try for elective office. Does John plan to run for elective office in the future? "Anything is possible," he says, although the conditions don't seem right for him to run anytime soon:

Running for office takes a special fire in the belly, and right now I don't have it. A candidate shouldn't be primarily motivated by ego, but by conviction and a focused approach to the issues. The voters are smart, and if you are not running for the right reasons, they will see right through you. For now, I will continue to work on affordable housing, and will volunteer when I think I can make a difference. In terms of seeking elective office again, the time is not right for me. But if I saw a true need in the future, I would consider doing it again.

Elective Office

As already stated, the over 500,000 elective positions in the United States offer substantial opportunities for political science graduates. The vast majority of elective positions are found at the state and local level. These include city council members, county board members, mayors, county commissioners, school board members, state representatives, treasurers, and secretaries of state. While many elective positions serve as the office holder's primary employment, many others are considered part time, to be fulfilled in addition to the elected official's primary career. This is the case for many local councils and county boards, and many state legislatures. For the most part elected officials are typical citizens who one day decided to run for office. While you don't need any special talent to run for and win office, the most successful candidates have a passion for public service and a commitment to work hard to pursue their agenda. Aspiring candidates must decide, first, if they want to pursue elective office for good reasons and, second, when is the right time to run. A political science degree can provide the aspiring office holder a basic understanding of government institutions, political process, and public policy. If you think you might be interested in pursuing electoral office in the future, you might try to get active in school government or in campus interest groups or club activities. You should also consider pursuing volunteer or internship opportunities in local campaigns, interest groups, government agencies, and political party organizations.

In most cases people serve for a number of years in lower office before they aspire to higher offices. For example, a college graduate with a few years of public or private sector work experience may get elected to a local council position and serve there for a number of years. She then might decide to run for the state legislature. After serving for a few terms in the legislature she might become a viable candidate for statewide office such as secretary of state, lieutenant governor, or even governor. Or, after serving in the state legislature she might consider running for national legislative offices such as a congressional representative or senator. Very rarely does a person successfully run for federal office without first serving in local or statewide office. The rare exceptions include millionaires who can finance their own campaigns, people who are already famous, or spouses of deceased congress members or senators.

Most elective positions offer low to moderate pay, and many require substantial commitments of time and energy. More than a few officeholders have retired from elective office after citing the strains of the job on themselves and their families. At the same time, many of our nation's founders, including Thomas Jefferson and George Mason, believed that the best elected representatives were those who served in office for a few years and then returned to private life. This vision of the "amateur" representative is still alive today; although the reality is that many elective offices attract political professionals who already have sufficient name recognition, political contacts and fundraising potential to mount a viable campaign.

Successfully running for office takes a huge amount of time and often a significant commitment of one's personal finances, among other personal resources. In addition, most aspiring office seekers must be willing to ask for monetary and volunteer support from others. Many candidates cite campaigning as one of the hardest things they have done. Yet most office seekers also look back fondly on their early campaigns when they and a few loyal friends and family members pulled off the monumental task of winning an election. Others who fell short of victory still feel an immense satisfaction in trying, and often try again and succeed.

Career Profile: Paul Wellstone

Paul Wellstone was a two-term Democratic Senator from Minnesota in a close race for reelection when he died in a plane crash along with his wife, their daughter, and five others on October 25, 2002. His rise from political science student and professor to maverick U.S. Senator offers one example of how much someone who is driven by conviction and a passion for public service can do.

Born on July 21, 1944, Wellstone was a professor of political science at Carleton College in Minnesota from 1969-1990. In 1990, he decided to challenge incumbent Republican Senator Rudy Boschwitz for election to the U.S. Senate. Although originally considered a hopeless underdog by many experts, Wellstone attract public attention by traveling the state in his green bus, and by airing offbeat campaign ads, one of which proclaimed, "I'm better looking." It is obvious now that Minnesotans were looking for a straight-talking candidate who wasn't afraid to shake up politics as usual to promote his liberal agenda. Wellstone confounded the skeptics by beating Boschwitz in a close contest, 50 percent to 48 percent.

As a freshman senator, Wellstone fought tirelessly for liberal causes including civil rights and opposition to oil development in Alaska. In describing his particular style and approach to office, CNN characterized Wellstone as "...combative and bold," but who "also had an easy smile and [who] often tried to inject humor into politics."[2] Even conservatives such as Senator Jesse Helms praised Wellstone for sticking to his convictions and maintaining his own style and approach to the job.

Wellstone wasn't content with merely studying politics. Instead, he took his extensive knowledge of politics and public policy and used it to reach out to his fellow Minnesotans, and to Americans across the country. A short time before his death, Wellstone reflected on his tenure in the Senate and his current reelection effort in an interview with CNN: "I really tried

to never do anything I don't believe in, so I don't want to change it now."
Whether you consider yourself a liberal or conservative, Democrat or
Republican (or none of these), Paul Wellstone's style and perseverance in
pursuing public service can be an inspiration to us all.

Additional Resources

- One World provides a list of world human rights organizations,
  found at <www.oneworld.net>.

- Alliance for Justice is a national association comprised of various
  groups including those involved in civil rights, consumer rights,
  women's health and environmental advocacy. Website information
  found at <www.afj.org>.

- Ecomall is a directory of grassroots environmental organizations.
  Go to <www.ecomall.com>.

- Points of Light Foundation brings people together for volunteer
  service in areas involving youth service and training. Found at
  <www.pointsoflight.org>.

- Republican National Committee, found at <www.rnc.org>.

- Democratic National Committee, found at <www.democrats.org>.

- The Libertarian Party, found at <www.lp.org>.

- The Green Party of the United States, found at <www.gp.org>.

- *Campaigns & Elections* magazine provides essential information
  about campaign opportunities, campaign manager and consultant
  services, campaign seminars and training opportunities, and a
  political job line. Found at <www.campaignline.com>.

---

[1] Interview with the author.
[2] Sean Loughlin, "Wellstone Made Mark as a Liberal Champion,"
CNN.com, 10-25-02. Biographical details were derived from Loughlin,

"Wellstone Made Mark," and Associated Press Biography of Paul Welstone, Minnesota Public Radio, 10-25-02, <news.mpr.org>.

13. Teaching

Teachers are vitally important for educating and socializing the next generation of citizens and leaders. Ask someone about their favorite teacher, and chances are they will quickly and enthusiastically recall one or more teachers who made a great impact on their life. Talk with a teacher about why they like teaching, and he or she will probably describe for you the profound reward of helping a young person "get it": whether it's a new math concept, the deeper meaning of a poem, or the value of hard work to attain one's goals.

Educators are among the most numerous government employees at the state and local level. Usually employed within a school district, educators at the primary, middle and secondary levels hold positions as teachers, school administrators, school counselors and librarians. Of the 3.8 million teachers in 2000, 598,000 taught preschool and kindergarten, 1.5 million taught elementary school, 590,000 taught middle school, and 1.1 million taught high school.[1] Teaching positions in state colleges and universities constitute approximately 30 percent of all state workers. [2]

Elementary, Middle, and Secondary School Teachers

Because elementary school[3] is where young people first learn to read, write, and do basic math, the role of elementary school teacher is vitally important in modern society. Elementary teachers are also instrumental in helping young people discover the world around them, and in developing good social and problem-solving skills. In many jurisdictions, elementary school includes grades one through six, while some public and private school districts include kindergarten, and possibly grades six, seven or eight. Elementary school teachers are topic generalists who are usually responsible for teaching math, science, social studies, and the language arts to a group of students that often ranges between 20 and 30 children. Some teachers may also be responsible for instruction in additional subjects such as art, music, or computers.

Middle school generally constitutes grades six through eight. Some districts still use the junior high school model, which may include grades seven, eight, and nine. Middle school teachers are often grouped in teams, with each teacher being responsible for one or more subjects including math, science, social studies, and language arts. Other team members might include teachers who teach specialty courses in art, foreign languages, and physical education.

High school teachers generally are topic specialists who teach in grades nine through twelve. Basic high school courses include English, social studies, government, history, mathematics, science, fine arts, foreign language, and physical education. Teachers at the high school level are usually grouped into departments, such as social studies, which may oversee various specific subjects including government, history, and geography. As with elementary and middle school teachers, high school teachers are instrumental in preparing young people to become responsible and productive members of society.

Obviously, teaching at all three levels involves more than just showing up and teaching classes. Teachers spend a lot of time and effort preparing lesson plans that are in keeping with curriculum guidelines, monitoring students' progress and providing feedback, and assigning grades on assignments and in quarterly reports. In addition, teachers must regularly interact with fellow teachers and school volunteers, principles and department heads, and parents. Such interaction often takes place in committees, meetings and conferences. Finally, since federal law mandates that special education students attend regular classes whenever possible, teachers often are responsible for providing individualized instruction to these special-needs students. Many teachers report having to work between 10 and 12 hours a day to complete their responsibilities, and often devote time on weekends to complete their work as well.

After teaching for a while, elementary, middle and secondary teachers may decide to pursue opportunities in school administration. Administrative positions include *department heads,* who also usually teach, *assistant principals*, *principals*, and district administrators including *curriculum specialists*, *program directors*, and *superintendents*.

To qualify for teaching, an individual must hold a bachelor's degree, and usually must attain a teaching certificate or master's degree within a limited time after obtaining a bachelor's degree. Those interested in pursuing a teaching career are advised to accrue exposure to the field through volunteer work, student teaching, or internships in the classroom.

Salaries and Employment Trends in Primary and Secondary Teaching

Most teachers don't expect to get rich in their profession. Those who stay in teaching over the long run usually cite their positive impact on young people as the job's greatest reward. At the same time, evidence suggests that teachers' salaries are getting better. According to the American Federation of Teachers, the average yearly salary of all elementary and secondary school teachers in 1999/2000 was $41,820, with beginning teachers holding bachelor's degrees earning on average $27,989 a year.

Opportunities for teaching in general are good to excellent in the next ten years as many current teachers are expected to retire, particularly at the secondary level. Teacher shortages will be greatest in states with large projected enrollments including California, Texas, Arizona and Georgia, while fewer teachers will be needed in areas with stagnating or declining enrollments including some states in the Midwest and Northeast. There will be less demand for social studies, government, and history teachers, and more for teachers in science, mathematics, foreign languages, and computer science. However, more teachers in all subjects will be needed in urban districts that often have large minority enrollments and overcrowded schools.

Graduates with a bachelor's degree can obtain teaching certificates or master's degrees in a university teaching program. In many states certified teachers must earn a master's degree within a specified period after being hired. Aspiring secondary school teachers generally major in the subject they plan to teach, and then complete post-graduate teacher training courses or programs of study. Universities and elementary, middle and high schools often partner to offer joint programs that include one year of teacher training followed by an internship, assistantship, or probationary teaching assignment. Political science graduates may seek endorsements to teach history, social studies and government at the secondary level, among other assignments. Prospective teachers in all fields who can also teach courses in computers, math, and languages are often more marketable than teacher candidates who don't have additional proficiency in those areas.

Career Profile: Russell Phipps

Russell Phipps is a Social Studies Specialist in the office of Instructional Services, Fairfax County Public Schools (FCPS), the largest school district in Virginia. Russ oversees curriculum and instructional development for all high school social studies teachers. His position requires that he keep current on the latest mandates from school administrators and government officials involving learning and instructional standards. According to Russ:

> I supervise a group of teachers on curriculum development involving the new Standards of Learning (SOLs). In response to the *No Child Left Behind Act*, I also work on remediation materials and summer courses for students who lag behind. On the instructional side, I plan workshops and training designed to help people become better teachers. I also work with new teachers. In total, I am responsible for about 700 teachers.[4]

While in college completing his double major in Government and History, Russ became very excited about the prospect of a career in teaching: "It was an epiphany for me, I really wanted it. As a student teacher I spent a lot of time writing lesson plans, and I couldn't wait to get back in the classroom the next day." Russ spent many years in high school classrooms teaching various subjects including history and government. He also served for a time as a social studies department chair, which essentially involves being a liaison between teachers and administrators. Reflecting back on when he started teaching in the 1960s, Russ sees some major changes in the profession between then and now:

> Teaching is different today compared to 25 years ago. Back then there was much less oversight and pressure, and more collegiality. You were questioned less by parents and administrators. Then in the 1970s teaching became more professional, with more accountability, assessments, and credentials. Now, with the SOLs and the *No Child Left Behind Act*, it takes more time to cover it all and be all things to all people. Yet, teachers today still love working with kids and in their disciplines. It remains first and foremost about kids for them. I also still love working with kids, and planting seeds, although

122

I'm not in the classroom anymore. It's especially
rewarding to receive letters from past students
who say they went into teaching because of me.

Another difference between then and now is the existence of various
programs today that are available to help students who want to teach.
These include masters programs in teaching where students take courses at
night and work in teaching internships during the day, and so-called "fifth-
year" programs where students earn a teaching credential or masters
degree at the end of their regular undergraduate studies. For those students
who are interested in exploring a teaching career, Russ recommends
learning as much as possible about the profession from actual teachers. He
also thinks there is no substitute for practical experience in the classroom
to see first-hand whether teaching is right for you.

Post-Secondary Teaching

College and university professors specialize in one academic discipline,
such as government, political science, or public administration, and
usually devote most of their research and teaching to one sub-field within
that discipline. Professors at the community college level generally hold at
least a master's degree, but many also hold doctoral degrees. Community
college professors typically teach three to four courses per semester, and
usually are responsible for advising students as well. Professors at two-
year schools are also expected to work on committees, and may be asked
by their department chair to oversee other special programs such as Model
UN, debate club, or the student honors society. Students at the community
college level vary widely in terms of their academic preparation and
reasons for attending school. Thus, community college professors must be
prepared to work with a diverse classroom of students with varying skills
and motivations to learn. Many community college administrators place
greater emphasis on teaching and advising when evaluating their
professors for promotions than research and other professional activities.

Full-time professors at the four-year college or university level generally
hold doctorates in political science. Like their colleagues at the
community college level, university professors typically are expected to
teach three to four courses a semester, and to provide service on campus
committees and special programs. However, university professors are also
expected to maintain an active program of research and scholarly writing.
While some of this research activity is conducted during sabbaticals or

123

periods of restricted teaching loads, university professors often must work nights and weekends to meet all of their obligations.

Salaries and Employment Trends in Post-Secondary Teaching
Earnings vary greatly among public and private colleges and universities. According to the American Association of University Professors (AAUP), full-time faculty at two-year colleges received average annual salaries ranging from $34,316 to $54,875, while average annual salaries for full-time instructors, as well as assistant, associate and full professors at all schools ranged from $31,411 to $83,207.[5] Part-time instructors at two-year and four-year schools make substantially less on average per course than full-time instructors. In political science courses, for example, a typical instructor will likely make between $2,500 and $5000 total per course. Undoubtedly, many of these part-time instructors are happy with their situation, as teaching for them may be a secondary career. However, many part-time instructors are qualified aspirants for full-time positions who haven't landed a job in the competitive employment market.

The average salaries for full-time professors are considered adequate for the amount of work and responsibilities faculty must complete. But for many professors the added benefits of tenure and the opportunities to do outside consulting make faculty positions particularly desirable. The term "tenure" means that someone who holds tenure is assured a job at her institution until she retires or resigns. A tenured professor cannot be fired except for just cause, which is very rare. To gain tenure a professor must produce a sufficient record of original research, community and professional service, and demonstrated excellence in teaching within five or six years of being hired. While fulfilling their full-time teaching, research, and service duties, many tenured and untenured professors also serve as paid consultants to public and private entities, which can substantially increase their base yearly salary. Full-time faculty also may receive money from their department or university for travel to scholarly conferences, or research stipends to pay research assistants.

Most recent studies predict significant growth in student enrollments at two and four-year colleges and universities over the next decade, but teaching budgets are not expected to keep pace with such growth. To address the increased budget constraints, college and university administrators are increasingly using part-time instructors to teach classes, also known as *adjunct professors*, while decreasing the number of new tenure-track hires. In fact, this trend has already started with the number of part-time faculty swelling from 22 percent of higher education teaching staffs in 1970, to 43 percent in 1999.[6] Therefore, while the number of students in two and four-year colleges and universities continues to rise, the competition for full teaching positions in political science and other social sciences is expected to become more acute.

Additional Resources

- *Career Opportunities in Education*, Echaore-McDavid, Susan. New York: Checkmark Books (2001).

- Recruiting New Teachers, Inc. based in Belmont, MA, is a national organization that helps people become teachers. Its website is found at <www.recruitingteachers.org>.

- A list of accredited teacher education programs is provided by the National Council for Accreditation of Teacher Education, at <www.ncate.org>.

- Other information about the teaching professions can be obtained by the American Federation of Teachers, at <www.aft.org>, or from the National Education association, at <www.nea.org>.

- American Association of University Professors, at <www.aaup.org>.

---

[1] U.S. Department of Labor statistics and teacher employment trends found at <www.bls.gov/oco/ocos069.htm>.

[2] Neale Baxter, *Opportunities in Government Careers*. Chicago: VGM Career Books (2001) p. 7.

[3] The following descriptions of elementary, secondary, and post-secondary teaching roles are derived from Susan Echaore-McDavid, *Career Opportunities in Education*. New York: Checkmark Books (2001), and Roy Edelfelt, *Careers in Education*. Chicago: VGM Career Horizons (1998).

[4] Interview with the author.

[5] Salary survey conducted in 1998-1999. Reported in Echaaore-McDavid, *Career Opportunities* (2001).

[6] Reported in Eric L. Wee, "Professor of Desperation," *The Washington Post Magazine* (7-21-02), p. 26.

14. Graduate Study

People enroll in graduate school for a variety of reasons. Some students enjoy their undergraduate learning experiences so much that they decide to continue in-depth studies in their undergraduate major, or in a different field in graduate school. Others attend graduate school because they think a graduate degree will improve their income potential. Still others pursue graduate degrees because they are necessary prerequisites for their chosen field of study, or are commonly associated with career advancement in that field. Finally, it's no secret to admissions officers that some people choose graduate school because they don't want to leave college. School is a comfortable place to be, so why leave now?

The first three reasons are probably sufficient to apply to graduate school, while the last is certainly an insufficient reason to do so. For those who choose graduate school for the right reasons, and can devote sufficient time and attention to their studies, graduate study can be a rewarding experience that will likely pay significant future dividends.

In this chapter the terms "graduate school" or "graduate study" will encompass masters and doctoral programs in the areas of liberal arts and humanities, social sciences (including political science and public administration), business and technical fields, and natural sciences. Law school programs that result in the juris doctorate degree are also included.

Some Differences Between Graduate and Undergraduate Programs
Graduate programs differ from undergraduate programs in several important ways. Graduate seminars tend to be smaller, more rigorous, and more focused on one subject for in-depth study. You will likely read more in a shorter period of time in graduate school than you ever did in school before. And since graduate programs are usually smaller and their admissions criteria more competitive, the students in your seminars will likely be more competitive too. In fact, some programs and individual professors encourage competition among students to in the hope of generate better work from everyone.

Graduate programs differ significantly in terms of their degree type, their specialization, and their prevailing models of learning. Like undergraduate programs, graduate programs are ranked against each other based on various criteria including overall reputation, publishing record of faculty, incoming student GPAs and admissions test scores, and the amount of money available to students for scholarships and research or teaching assistantships.

Many people who hire for private and public sector positions place a lot of importance on a particular graduate program's ranking. Academic departments that are looking to hire a new full time professor, for example, will put considerable emphasis on the ranking and reputation of their job candidates' graduate schools. Other career sectors place less emphasis on program rankings, and will likely consider your graduate degree a plus no matter where you attended. (This assumes your degree is from an accredited school.) A middle manager in a state agency, for example, is less apt to be swayed by graduate school rankings in evaluating applicants for a staff position in his office. Instead, he may compare all applicants who hold graduate degrees on their relevant work experience and overall "fit" for the position.

Types of Graduate Programs
The number and types of graduate programs in the United States have expanded greatly in the last few decades. In addition to the more traditional programs in the liberal arts, humanities, and the social and hard sciences, nontraditional degree programs in a variety of specialties are opening in areas including conflict resolution, gender studies, nonprofit management, and diplomacy. Many programs also offer alternative scheduling options for students including cohort, weekend, and online programs.

Despite the proliferation of degree types and formats, three general models of graduate programs are most prevalent:[1]

Coursework and thesis programs at the master's level usually require one to two years of formal seminar work followed by a thesis project that takes an additional one or two years to complete. These programs usually require students to first complete qualifying exams in one or more fields of study within their major. Students who fail the exams in one or more tries may be dismissed from the program. Ph.D. programs almost always include rigorous qualifying exams (written, oral, or both) before students advance to the dissertation stage. Many doctoral programs also require students to write a formal dissertation proposal that must be approved by their dissertation committee before the student is considered ABD (which stands for "all but dissertation"). The average time a student takes to complete a master's or doctoral thesis varies greatly among disciplines, and may even vary among sub-field within disciplines. For example, a political science doctoral dissertation in normative political theory may take longer to complete than a dissertation in an empirically driven sub-specialty like formal theory or voting behavior.

Coursework and exam programs allow students to forgo the thesis option in favor of comprehensive exams (given orally or in writing, or both). This option usually doesn't apply to doctoral programs. Coursework and exam programs often require students to take more courses, and may maintain higher expectations for their student's test performance. Law programs are generally based on this model as well. Since many graduate students stall or even drop out at the thesis stage, the coursework and exam model may be the right choice for students who are working full time and going to school part time.

Coursework and internship models are usually found in clinical or applied graduate programs including teaching, social work, and counseling. These programs may still require students to complete a round of comprehensive exams, and perhaps a thesis or extensive research paper, but the emphasis is generally on the internship as the culminating evaluative experience.

In trying to gain acceptance under a competitive process, applicants for graduate school face a formidable hurdle that can stress out even the most even-tempered and efficient persons. The basic steps include: researching and choosing schools where you will apply; preparing for and taking the required standardized test; securing letters of recommendation; drafting and polishing a personal statement (required for many, but not all programs); and filling out the myriad program forms including financial aid and scholarship applications.

These basic steps are examined in more detail below.[2] Before you think about how to apply to graduate school you should think carefully about whether graduate school is the right choice for you.

Is Graduate School Right for You?
While more people than ever are attending graduate school, graduate study is not for everyone. You should first think seriously about whether graduate school is right for you, and if so whether now is the right time to

apply. Do you have a particular career sector in mind that requires a graduate degree to start (e.g., practicing law) or to advance beyond a particular point (e.g., nonprofit management)? If your desired career field doesn't require graduate training for entry or even middle-level positions, you might consider delaying the start of graduate school until you are sure you want to remain in that career field. By working for a few years you might have a better idea about what you want from graduate school, and a better understanding of how to get it.

Some graduate admissions officials value a candidate's work experiences beyond the four-year degree. By logging a few years of practical work experience you may become a stronger candidate. Also, as a salaried employee of a public or private organization you may qualify for tuition assistance to help offset the costs of your graduate education. Employers are increasingly willing to invest in their employees' continuing education and in many cases will offer flexible work hours so you can attend classes.

Who can help you evaluate whether graduate school is right for you? For starters, talk with your professors, especially those in the fields you are interested in pursuing further. Ask them about the careers associated with specific graduate degrees, and their opinion on the pros and cons of attending graduate school to attain your goals. You may also want to talk with your current employer and even other professionals in your desired career field. Try to get a sense of how much they would value pursuing a graduate degree now versus working to gain further on-the-job experience.

You should also make an appointment with the program coordinators in several graduate programs you are considering. If a personal visit is impractical, try to engage them in conversation over the phone. Program coordinators can provide information about the program's strengths and specific requirements and about the types of students currently enrolled. They may even provide the current names of students you can speak with. Increasingly, graduate programs offer "virtual tours" on their websites that promote each program's strengths and particular offerings. Such tours can be quite helpful for narrowing down your range of options to consider.

Choosing the Right Program for You
Once you decide that graduate school is the right choice, you will need to systematically explore your available options. Because new programs of various types are constantly being developed, choosing a short list of

places where you will apply is more complicated than you think. Once again, your professors are probably the best initial source of information about the programs that you are considering.

Overall program rankings will be a key determinant for many students. Besides students who are seeking professional degrees in law or medicine, those who aspire to teach at four-year colleges or universities should place a program's overall ranking in their primary list of considerations. Among the various sources for graduate school rankings is *U.S. News and World Report*, which publishes an annual ranking of graduate schools in most fields. Graduate programs are compared on various criteria including number of faculty, quality of admitted students as measured by standardized tests, research dollars generated by the faculty, and scholarship support available to students.

While national rankings are helpful in identifying a range of program possibilities, they are no substitute for more in-depth comparisons by you. In comparing programs be sure to explore questions such as: How many courses must you complete? Are you required to complete comprehensive examinations? Are you required to write a thesis? Are there opportunities for internships, fieldwork, research assistantships or other forms of faculty and student collaboration? How many graduate degrees are awarded each year? How long on average do students take to complete the degree? What percent of students enter the program but fail to finish? How many faculty teach in the graduate program? What is the student-to-teacher ratio in a typical seminar? Are faculty assigned to students as advisors or mentors, or do they just teach the courses? What percent of graduate faculty are tenured versus part-time adjuncts? Does the program help students with job placement support?

You might weigh other variables including location of the program. For example, is the program located in a place where you want to spend the next three or four years? If you are a "city person," you should think seriously before attending a program in rural area. Whenever possible, it's always better to visit potential schools personally in order to see the facilities first-hand, and hopefully to talk with some of the faculty and students.

Preparing Your Application Materials
Once you identify a list of schools to closely consider, you should call, email, or write to them requesting a catalog, application materials, and financial aid forms. You can also use these materials to make further comparisons. Graduate application forms can be quite lengthy and usually require detailed information about your prior schools attended, your work experience and extracurricular activities, and your (and sometimes your parent's) financial status if you are applying for any type of scholarship, assistantship, or loan. If you are applying for federal or state student loans, you will also have to complete the lengthy Free Application for Federal Student Aid (FAFSA) form.

As you review each program's application materials, pay particular attention to the application deadlines for each program. Application deadlines vary widely, even among different programs at the same school. To be considered for financial aid, scholarships, or assistantships applicants generally must submit all application materials a month or more prior to the general admissions deadline.

Standardized Entrance Exams
Most accredited graduate programs require applicants to submit scores from a standardized exam. As soon as possible determine first whether you need to take a standardized admissions test, and the exact test required. Some programs may allow you to forgo the admissions test if your undergraduate GPA is above a certain level, which varies from program to program. (This is one good reason why you should strive to do well in your undergraduate classes!) Other programs will require completion of the appropriate standardized test no matter how high your undergraduate GPA. The standardized tests required for most programs include the following:

Graduate Record Examination (GRE): This exam is required by a variety of graduate programs in the humanities, liberal arts, and social sciences (including political science). Scores on the GRE are determined by your answers to multiple-choice questions grouped into verbal (reading comprehension, vocabulary skill) and analytical sections (mathematics through simple geometry and formal logic problems). Some programs also require applicants to take a subject-area test.

Law School Admissions Test (LSAT): The LSAT is used for law school admissions. It consists of multiple-choice questions in sections testing reading comprehension, analytical reasoning, and logical reasoning. A 30-minute writing sample is also administered at the end of the test. The Law School Admissions Council does not score the sample, but copies are sent to all law schools to which you apply.

Graduate Management Admissions Test (GMAT): The GMAT is used by most business and management programs. Like the GRE and LSAT, it tests verbal, quantitative and analytical skills. Unlike the other two, the GMAT's analytical section requires two essays.

You cannot effectively "study for" these tests in the traditional sense. At the same time, it pays to familiarize yourself with the question types, the scoring method used, and some widely accepted test-taking strategies. If you can afford it you should seriously consider taking a preparation course offered by a reputable test preparation service including Kaplan or Princeton Review. These courses can be expensive, but evidence suggests that if you practice their techniques and complete several practice tests you can significantly raise your score. Short of enrolling in prep courses, you can purchase or borrow from your library one of the test preparation books that are written for your specific exam. Be sure to complete one or more practice tests that are widely available.

GPA Transcripts
Most schools require official transcripts from all schools you attended beyond high school. Admissions officials will look for solid evidence that you have the academic skills and work ethic to do well in their program. Towards this end they may place more emphasis on grades earned in academically rigorous courses such as constitutional law for law school applicants and quantitative methods for political science applicants interested in studying formal political methods.

Generally, your cumulative GPA is considered your official GPA. The cumulative GPA is calculated from the grades you earned in all courses you ever took, even those you failed or didn't apply towards your undergraduate degree. For students with uneven academic records (e.g., students who "failed out" one semester early in their academic careers), admissions officials may compare your cumulative GPA with your work in the last two years of study. This takes into account students who were not ready to do well in college or who experienced unexpected personal problems.

While GPA is important, it's not the only thing admissions officials take into account. Most graduate programs seek "well rounded" students who have done more in their lives than study hard and get good grades. Do you have significant work experience? Are you active in community affairs? Do you have advanced skills? Have you traveled extensively or lived in another country? These may be considered positive factors, but you must present them in the best light to get credit. This is where the personal essay can make the difference.

Personal Essays

Many graduate programs require applicants to write a personal essay or statement of purpose as part of their application materials. If done well these statements can effectively offset certain weaknesses in your background or credentials, and in some cases can get you accepted even though you are not an "automatic accept."

Beyond the obvious opportunity to show you can write well, a strong essay can do other things for you. Your essay should make the case that you are someone who will not only get good grades, but who will also make a significant contribution to the quality of the seminars and the overall program. For example, students who lived in other countries or who have extensive work experience in international affairs may be particularly desirable to admissions officials in a master's program in international relations. Your personal statement can also help explain why your GPA is not as high as it should be. For example, a single mother who had to work full time while going to school may gain admission even though her other credentials are lower than the applicant pool's average.

Your statement is only as good as the effort you put into it. Many applicants delay drafting their statements until near the application deadline, and it shows. To get it just right you should expect to spend many hours on your personal statement. You should also provide a draft of your statement when you ask professors or others to write you a letter of recommendation. This will help them incorporate more details about you in their letters and may help reinforce your particular strengths as a candidate.

Letters of Recommendation

Most graduate schools require at least two letters of recommendation from professors or others who can speak knowledgeably about your academic skills and personal attributes. If you diligently cultivated your contacts among the professors who teach your classes you will be positioned to request and secure good letters. On the other hand, if you haven't made the effort to get to know your professors and, more importantly, given your professors a chance to know you it will be more difficult to get good letters.

Your professors are asked to write scores of recommendation letters in a given year. Usually they will provide standard mediocre praise for most students, and reserve their strongest letters for only their best students, or for those students they know well enough to promote their strengths and explain their weaknesses. If you ask someone to write you a letter and they seem hesitant to do so, or indicate the recommendation will be a mediocre one, you should seek someone else's help. To maximize your chances of receiving a strong letter of recommendation, be sure to follow the basic protocol:

- Give your letter writer plenty of advanced notice, and be clear about the final deadline.

- Provide your letter writer a copy of your draft statement, a resume, and, if requested, any prior academic work submitted to their class or other classes. . It's also a good idea to hand deliver these materials, if possible, so your professor can connect a face with your name.

- Provide all required forms and self-addressed and stamped envelopes.

Non-Teaching Positions Requiring Advanced Degrees

Besides teaching, a graduate degree in political science or related major such as public administration can enhance your opportunities in the applied research field. Middle and upper positions in government often require an advanced degree. For example, a master's degree in political science or related fields including public administration or public policy is considered a necessity for most county or city managers, directors of nonprofit organizations, and political directors of interest groups. Most professional pollsters and political consultants also hold advanced degrees.

A Ph.D. is generally considered a prerequisite for applied researchers employed in so-called "think tanks." *Think tanks* are nonprofit groups engaged in research that is of interest to governments and policymakers at all levels, and others including nonprofit and business managers. Examples of prominent think tanks include the Brookings Institute, Progressive Policy Institute, CATO Institute, American Enterprise Institute, and the RAND Corporation. Generally, scholars who work at think tanks already hold faculty positions at a college or university. Thus, there are few positions at think tanks for graduates who first don't pursue the teaching route.

Additional Resources

- An online version of the Free Application for Federal Student Aid is found at
  <www.fafsa.ed.gov>.

- The American Political Science Association website, at <www.apsanet.org>, includes an overview of graduate programs in political science and related disciplines, a database of scholarships for graduate study, and updates on the work of the APSA Task Force on Graduate Education in Political Science.

- *US News and World Report's* "America's Best Graduate Schools" is be found at
  <www.usnews.com>.

There are several educational testing and products services that also provide good initial advice about all facets of graduate study. These include:

- The College Board, at <www.collegeboard.com>.

- Law School Admissions Council, at <www.lsac.org>.

- Petersons, at <www.petersons.com>.

- Princeton Review, at <www.princetonreview.com>.

- Kaplan, at <www.kaplan.com>.

---

[1] The following information is derived from materials provided at the 25th Annual Graduate & Professional School Fair of Washington DC Area Universities, held at George Washington University, September 2002. For more information about graduate admissions, school rankings, and the great diversity of program offerings in graduate and law schools, go to <www.gradfair.gwu.edu>.

[2] In addition to drawing on the author's personal experiences in advising undergraduates, this information was compiled from various web resources including <www.wartburg.edu/careers/gradschool.html>, <www.gradfair.gwu.edu>, and <www.careerbuilder.com>.

15. Additional Strategies for Success

Careers in Political Science has provided you a basic overview of the career fields open to political science majors. You should have a better sense of the vast range of career options available to you, and a better understanding of the particular skills, challenges and rewards associated with different career fields. You also have a set of resources to further explore potential career fields in more detail. This final chapter discusses additional strategies for educational and career success. While all of these strategies won't work for everyone in every situation, if you practice as many as possible you are sure to get more out of your undergraduate program, and will likely avoid many common mistakes that other students make in preparing for their future careers.

GPA and Educational Success
What constitutes educational success for one person may be different for another. Your grade point average (GPA) is just one measure of educational achievement, but it's an important one. A strong GPA can open doors and help you keep your options open, while a weak GPA can foreclose future possibilities. Whether you plan to attend graduate school in the future or not, you should earn a sufficiently high GPA to keep that option open for yourself. You don't want to find out later that your GPA is too low to get into a good program, or any program for that matter.

By maintaining a high GPA you may also compete for scholarships or other forms of merit awards later in your undergraduate program. Although freshman scholarships are the most publicized, many schools, organizations, and foundations offer limited scholarships or awards to students in their junior or senior years. These scholarships are less publicized, and therefore less competitive. Students with a GPA of at least 3.5 or above can usually compete for these awards, while students with lower GPAs usually cannot. Scholarship awards are also good resume builders for job searches and graduate school applications.

Why do some students do very well in their classes, while others struggle? There are many factors associated with educational success. Some factors, such as intelligence, are largely predetermined. Others are more subject to your control. For most students, success in school hinges on fostering good learning habits and maintaining a strong work ethic. The following tips can help you be a better student, and ultimately a better employment prospect.

Required Reading
Professors assign readings with the expectation that you will complete them when they want you to. Unfortunately, many students don't read much, and it shows. If you conscientiously strive to complete your reading assignments, you will be ahead of those students who don't. Your professors' lectures will make more sense, and you will be better able to participate in class discussions and activities. By developing good reading habits in college, you are also preparing yourself for the increased demands of the workplace. Most careers discussed in this book require a lot of reading and quick comprehension. So get in the habit of reading every day; it will pay big dividends for you in the future.

This is not to say that you should read everything with equal thoroughness. During some weeks in the semester you will be overwhelmed with your many class commitments. Sometimes you will need to prioritize your readings in response to cues from your professors about what they think is most important. This is not the time to let your important priorities slip, or give up altogether. Instead, you must cope with the extra workload by tackling immediate deadlines first, while also maintaining your other, less pressing work. The key to this type of "multi-tasking" is to not let any course requirements go completely. Even if you can just scan a chapter over breakfast before lecture or read the chapter summary, you will get more out of your classes than if you never opened the book at all.

Exams
While many students consider all-night "cram sessions" before exams an inevitable part of the college experience, this method of test preparation is obviously not the most effective. Good test preparation involves early and active reading of assigned materials, and regular review of your lecture notes. Exam preparation is best done in blocks of time of between one and two hours. Be sure to schedule periods of time away from the television and ringing telephones, so you can pay total attention to what you are doing. This method is also more effective than studying with groups of students who prefer to talk about other things than the material or project at hand.

After your exam is graded and returned, you should make an appointment to meet with your professor to discuss how you can improve on the next exam. Believe it or not, your professors want you to do well, and most are willing to help you if you show initiative and a willingness to work.

Writing Skills

Have you noticed that virtually all the career fields discussed in this book require good writing skills? Despite the rapid changes currently taking place in various career sectors, good writing remains at or near the top of skills valued by employers. This is especially true for the careers most associated with political science. Unfortunately, many college students write poorly, and few seem willing to make a serious effort to improve. As a consequence, employers frequently complain that their new hires can't write, while the new hires have to scramble to improve on the job or risk missing out on promotions and other opportunities for advancement.

Good writing is not an inherited trait. It is a craft that must be learned, and that requires meticulous polishing over several drafts. Ask good writers how they produce excellent prose, and most will confirm that it's hard work. Once you accept this fact, you can begin correcting your own writing flaws. Don't just ignore the bad marks you receive on your papers; do something about them.

There are several things you can do to improve your writing skills. First, you can take more writing classes. Most college or university-level students must pass an introductory course in writing composition. But many students can benefit from taking more advanced writing classes as well. Instead of using all your electives for fun courses like Golf 101 or The History of Rock and Roll, set aside a few courses to develop your marketable skills, including strong writing. You might even consider adding an English minor. It will not only help you become a better writer, but will likely strengthen your resume as well.

Second, be sure to utilize the services at your campus's writing center. Most schools now have a full writing center on campus that serves students in all majors. This is an indication that your school administrators understand that you might need additional help. Writing centers typically offer writing workshops, handouts on a variety of writing subjects, and consultations with tutors who can review your writing assignments before you turn them in.

Finally, you can improve your writing by starting your writing assignments early enough to leave ample time for drafting and polishing. A lot of students with decent writing skills turn in shoddy assignments because they don't leave sufficient time to produce quality work. Their essays show promise, but they fall short because of poor organization, flawed grammar, and too many typographical errors that should never appear in an era of "spell and grammar check."

Getting to Know Your Professors
In the "old days" college students and their professors interacted more. Many programs in the past required students to meet with their faculty advisor each semester, and professors expected a visit from students who did poorly on their exams. Today most students rarely if ever meet with their professors. While this is not always the student's fault (some professors are simply not available very much), the student is the one who gets shortchanged.

Make a point to visit each of your course professors at least once during the semester. There are several benefits that can result. First, your professors will generally respond favorably to you and your work if you show that you are interested in the course material and are genuinely concerned about learning. While this has not been empirically tested, anecdotal evidence suggests that most professors are inclined to give you the benefit of the doubt in cases of borderline grades or other close judgement calls when they see you are making a concerted effort to meet their expectations. This doesn't mean you are "kissing up" to the professor. Instead, you are simply employing good learning practices such as clarifying a point that was made during a lecture, or requesting a review of the last exam so you can improve the next time around.

Go back and revisit those professors who seem willing to help you do better on exams and other course requirements, or who are interested in your educational or career aspirations. These professors can be invaluable to you later on when you are applying for scholarships, graduate schools, or jobs. Your best letters of recommendation will come from those professors who actually know you and can speak knowledgably about your personal and academic strengths.

Seeking Academic Advice

In addition to regular visits with your professors, you should meet periodically with your academic advisor to make sure you are on track with your general education and political science courses. Don't assume that you completely understand all your requirements for graduation. More than a few students who thought they were graduating found out too late that they were short a course or two. Don't let this happen to you. Most political science departments have designated academic advisors who can help you stay on track as well as provide additional information about minors, merit awards and scholarships, and special programs including internships and study abroad opportunities.

Exploring Your Career Goals While You Are in School

The last semester of your senior year is not the time to start thinking about life after school. On the contrary, the most successful students know how to develop their future career options during the several years they are in school. Your political science education offers many opportunities to explore potential careers. This book has discussed numerous positive things you can do to prepare earlier for career success such as using internships to gain workplace experience and to try out prospective career fields, and by taking certain course to enhance your marketable skills.

Other things you can do now to prepare yourself for a satisfying career later including career interviewing and networking, setting realistic goals, and maintaining a positive attitude and strong work ethic.

Career Networking and Interviewing

Career networking is the exchange of information with others for mutual benefit. Successful people constantly network with other successful people to find out about job openings, and to better compete for those opportunities. Your career network can start with fellow students in your classes, with contacts you make through your extra-curricular activities, and with your professors, coworkers, and supervisors. Your campus career center is also a good place to gain networking contacts either through the counselors who are available for career consultations, or through your school's alumni who might be available to talk with students about their careers.

Career interviews[1] are a useful tool to begin developing your networking contacts. Basically, a career interview is where you meet with someone to discuss what he or she does, and how you might prepare yourself for a position in their field. Who are good candidates for career interviews? Your academic department's alumni are a good start. Ask your professors or academic advisor about your program's alumni. Also check to see if your campus career center has an organized career interview program.

Career interviewing can seem awkward at first, but it's well worth it. Most people feel uncomfortable when they first ask someone to talk with them about their personal situation. You just have to remind yourself that career interviews are a widely accepted practice, and that you have nothing to lose from being a bit assertive.

Once you set up your appointment, prepare yourself to make the most of it. Try to learn about your contact's workplace and general career sector so you don't ask questions that you can easily answer through research. Also, by doing a bit of research before the interview you can ask more pointed questions during the interview. Some possible questions might include:

How did you get into this career field?
What is your typical day like?
What do you like about your job? What don't you like?
Where do you see yourself in five years?
What do employers look for in new hires?
Are there related fields that I should explore?
What positions might I now be qualified for?
Do you know anyone else who might be able to provide additional insights?
What additional skills should I work to develop?

During career interviews it's acceptable to ask about your qualifications for an entry-level position. It is not acceptable to ask your contact directly for a job. Your contact knows why you are there, and if there is a job opening he or she will likely raise the possibility of your applying for it. If your contact does mention a job opening, then it's okay for you to tactfully learn as much about that position during your meeting.

At the meeting's conclusion thank your contact and be sure to get his or her business card. Also make sure you send a thank you note within a day or two. If your contact gave you the names of others whom you should contact, make sure you follow up and call those contacts.

Maintaining a Positive Attitude and a Strong Work Ethic
While good skills and work experiences are essential to career success, equally important are good people skills and a consistent willingness to pitch in and do your fair share of the work, and sometimes even more. Your employers will expect you to prove yourself on smaller things before they give you more responsibility. It is very important that you handle these basic assignments efficiently and thoroughly, and without complaint. If you maintain a positive attitude and consistently do a good job, your supervisors will eventually notice and you will be given more challenging tasks. As Susan Oglinsky explains, "it's okay to challenge yourself and to set high goals, but you must realize that to attain your goals it takes little steps." [2]

Another key to success is to be realistic about your worth to the organization, and modest in your interactions with others. Believe it or not, whether you went to Harvard or to State University won't matter much once you graduate and start work. Too often new graduates from elite universities (and some not-so-elite universities) enter the workplace believing that they are superior to their peers, and too good for the mundane tasks new hires are often assigned. Those employees who complain about their work assignments often gain a negative reputation that is almost impossible to dispel. Do not follow their lead.

No matter where you went to school, it always pays to treat others with respect, even those employees with less education who occupy lower positions than yours. This is what Simonas Girdzijauskas learned in his internship and entry-level position in international affairs. His advice is to "pay attention to everyone, even the so-called 'little people.' Don't ignore the office secretaries and other support staff, and never burn your bridges. They are the ones who help you do your job better. And besides, it's just the right thing to do." [3]

Finally, whatever your short and long term career goals may be, in the short run you should always maintain your loyalty to your current supervisors and organization. Keep in mind that you were hired to advance the interests and mission of your workplace, not to promote your own self-interest. Therefore, it's best to work for someone or something that you believe in, and can wholeheartedly support. If you find that you fundamentally disagree with the values of your workplace, it's time to look for another job. Finding a job that reinforces your personal values

145

takes persistence, but the effort is well worth it. As Pat Lewis explains, "the time to examine these issues is before you actually accept the position. I like to see applicants who take the time to read the organization's mission statement, and who ask about the organization's long-term vision and how they might fit in. What employers are looking for are team players who can share that vision."[4]

Now that you have reviewed the various career possibilities that are open to political science majors, it might be helpful to reexamine your short and long-term career goals in relation to the personal and work values you identified in Chapter 2. As you continue to explore your future career path, be open to new ways of thinking and unexpected opportunities. And remember, a fulfilling career is never gained in a day. As Francis Bacon once said: "All rising to great places is by a winding stair."

Good luck.

---

[1] This discussion of career interviews is derived from Joel Clark, *Intern to Success*. Boston: Houghton Mifflin (2002).
[2] Interview with the author.
[3] Interview with the author.
[4] Interview with the author.

Index

NOTES

NOTES

NOTES

NOTES

NOTES

NOTES

NOTES